The Hong Kong Economic Policy Studies Series

IMMIGRATION AND
THE ECONOMY
OF HONG KONG

IMMIGRATION AND THE ECONOMY OF HONG KONG

Kit Chun Lam
Pak Wai Liu

Published for
The Hong Kong Centre for Economic Research
The Better Hong Kong Foundation
The Hong Kong Economic Policy Studies Forum
by

City University of Hong Kong Press

First published 1998
Printed in Hong Kong

ISBN 962-937-019-0

Published by
City University of Hong Kong Press
City University of Hong Kong
Tat Chee Avenue, Kowloon, Hong Kong

Internet: http://www.cityu.edu.hk/upress/
E-mail: upress@cityu.edu.hk

The free-style calligraphy on the cover, *yi,* means "migration" in Chinese.

Contents

Detailed Chapter Contents

Foreword

The key to the economic success of Hong Kong has been a business and policy environment which is simple, predictable and transparent. Experience shows that prosperity results from policies that protect private property rights, maintain open and competitive markets, and limit the role of the government.

The rapid structural change of Hong Kong's economy in recent years has generated considerable debate over the proper role of economic policy in the future. The impending restoration of sovereignty over Hong Kong from Britain to China has further complicated the debate. Anxiety persists as to whether the pre-1997 business and policy environment of Hong Kong will continue.

During this period of economic and political transition in Hong Kong, various interested parties will be re-assessing Hong Kong's existing economic policies. Inevitably, some will advocate an agenda aimed at altering the present policy making framework to reshape the future course of public policy.

For this reason, it is of paramount importance for those familiar with economic affairs to reiterate the reasons behind the success of the economic system in the past, to identify what the challenges are for the future, to analyze and understand the economy sector by sector, and to develop appropriate policy solutions to achieve continued prosperity.

In a conversation with my colleague Y. F. Luk, we came upon the idea of inviting economists from universities in Hong Kong to take up the challenge of examining systematically the economic policy issues of Hong Kong. An expanding group of economists (The Hong Kong Economic Policy Studies Forum) met several times to give form and shape to our initial ideas. The Hong Kong Economic Policy Studies Project was then launched in 1996 with some 30 economists from the universities in Hong Kong and a few from overseas. This is the first time in Hong Kong history that a concerted public effort has been undertaken by academic economists in the territory. It represents a joint expression of our collective concerns, our hopes for a better Hong Kong, and our faith in the economic future.

The Hong Kong Centre for Economic Research is privileged to be co-ordinating this Project. We are particularly grateful to The Better Hong Kong Foundation whose support and assistance has made it possible for us to conduct the present study, the results of which are published in this monograph. We also thank the directors and editors of the City University of Hong Kong Press and The Commercial Press (H.K.) Ltd. for their enthusiasm and dedication which extends far beyond the call of duty. The unfailing support of many distinguished citizens in our endeavour and their words of encouragement are especially gratifying.

Yue-Chim Richard Wong
Director
The Hong Kong Centre
for Economic Research

Foreword by the Series Editor

It is common knowledge that Hong Kong is a society of immigrants. A large proportion of its residents have come from elsewhere. In particular, immigrants from the Mainland provinces of China make up a major segment of society, currently accounting for over 30 percent of the population. Throughout the past 50 years, there has been significant synergy between immigrants from the Mainland and the development of the Hong Kong economy.

The population of Hong Kong increased rapidly after the Second World War. This increase has been largely caused by inflows of immigrants from Guangdong and other regions of China. Yet, the sharp rise of population has not impeded economic growth in Hong Kong at all. Instead, immigrants has supplied the much needed labour force for Hong Kong's miraculous economic growth.

What are the salient socio-economic characteristics of the Mainland immigrants — education background, productivity, and labour force participation ratio? Are there significant differences between earlier and recent immigrants? Given their large numbers, how have they affected the local labour market in respect of wages, job opportunities and income distribution? How have they performed individually as employers and as employees?

Answers to these questions are necessary for our good understanding of Hong Kong: of its labour market in particular and of its economy and society as a whole. It is the purpose of this book to deal with these issues in analytical depth.

Immigrants are not just a productive labour "input" in economic activities. They are individuals from families and their inflow entails many changes to human relations in both Hong Kong and the communities where they come from. All Hong Kong residents, as well as potential immigrants, are directly and indirectly influenced by our immigration policy.

Immigration from the Mainland is defined by an immigration policy stipulated by agreements between the Hong Kong Special Administration Region and the Mainland. Changes in immigration policy would affect directly the socio-economic characteristics of immigrants to Hong Kong, which would in turn affect the role of immigrants in the local economy. This book investigates the prevailing immigration policy from the point of view of the economic development of Hong Kong. Some concrete proposals for improvement of the policy are made.

The authors of this book, Professors Lam Kit Chun and Liu Pak Wai, are scholars in labour economics. They have done a lot of research and published many studies on immigration and the Hong Kong labour market. Their understanding of the issues is thorough and their arguments are based on economic theory and empirical evidence. This book is an authoritative study and is a necessary reference for informed discussion on the subject.

Y. F. Luk
School of Economics and Finance
The University of Hong Kong

Preface

The publication of this monograph is made possible by the financial support of the Better Hong Kong Foundation and the Hong Kong Centre for Economic Research (HKCER). Without HKCER Director Professor Richard Wong's unflagging effort to put together the Hong Kong Economic Policy Studies Series and without his prodding us to write on the topic of immigration, this monograph will not have come to fruition.

This monograph is based on research on immigration in Hong Kong, which we have been conducting over the last five years. The first half of Chapter 7 is based on results from a research project funded by the Research Grants Council. Chapter 8 is derived from a research project funded by a direct grant from Hong Kong Baptist University. Research assistance for the entire monograph has been provided by the Hong Kong and Asia-Pacific Economies Research Programme of the Institute of Asia-Pacific Studies, The Chinese University of Hong Kong. The Department of Census and Statistics of the Government of the Hong Kong Special Administrative Region has been very helpful in providing statistical data. The support of these institutions is gratefully acknowledged. We would also like to thank Professor Ma Lin, Mr. S. S. Yeung and Ms. Pansy Ho for their valuable comments and suggestion.

We would like to express our appreciation of Mr. Chan Chi-sing for his able research assistance and to Mrs. Aileen Choi, who has patiently and efficiently gone over several drafts of the monograph.

Last but not least, we would like to thank our daughters, **Wendy** and **Carol,** for their forbearance during the past year, when we were engaged in the writing of this monograph. To them this monograph is dedicated.

Kit Chun Lam
Pak Wai Liu
November 1997

List of Illustrations

Figures

Tables

CHAPTER 1

Introduction

Hong Kong is a society of immigrants. In 1996, 32.6% of its population were immigrants from Mainland China (hereafter called the Mainland). Another 7.1% of the population were born in places other than China or Hong Kong. Most of this 7.1% is made up of expatriate employees and their dependents, foreign workers, and domestic helpers. In total, people born outside Hong Kong make up almost 40% of Hong Kong's population, as compared, for example, with the United States, where 9.3% of the population is foreign-born. Among the 60% of the population in Hong Kong who are natives, most have parents or grandparents who are immigrants.

Immigrants are self-selected with respect to hard-work, determination to better life, and willingness to take risks. Over the years, these qualities have shaped the ethos and values of Hong Kong society. They are the driving force that has made Hong Kong so successful. It is not an exaggeration to say that immigrant blood flows in the veins of the people of Hong Kong.

In early days Hong Kong was open to immigrants in China. Many came to the territory to escape Communist rule. Almost everyone was poor at that time. Immigrants worked hard to eke out a living in a backward colony teeming with refugees looking for work. However, those already in Hong Kong did not reject newcomers, for they themselves were sojourners hoping one day to return to their home villages in the Mainland.

After decades of economic growth, Hong Kong has prospered enormously. It has taken its place among the advanced countries as ranked by per capita Gross Domestic Product (GDP). The immigrant society has come of age and transformed itself. Some immigrants have succeeded beyond their wildest dreams of accumulating enormous wealth, while many others have at least become financially secure. Their affinity for Hong Kong grows with time. Their second and third generations are Hong Kong belongers, planting deep roots and taking Hong Kong as their permanent home. The sojourner mentality has faded, and a Hong Kong identity is established.

As Hong Kong's immigrant society comes of age, it is beginning to close in much the same way that the societies of mature immigrant nations like the United States and Australia have closed. Successful immigrants and their children and grandchildren are eager to protect their way of life and their standard of living. Segments of the community begin to see new immigrants at best as unwelcome guests and at worst as threats. Those who are already established become hostile to immigration and wish to reduce the flow of immigrants.

As a community of immigrants, Hong Kong people should be reminded of their immigrant origin. They should take appropriate stock of their immigrant experience and consider the contribution to the economy by past and prospective immigrants. Helping Hong Kong people to do this is the first objective of this book.

Nineteen ninety-seven was a historical year for Hong Kong. The end of British rule and the reunification with China have eliminated the political constraints governing Hong Kong's immigration policy. Many challenges have presented themselves as a result. The first and foremost among these is that of how to admit into Hong Kong the Mainland-born children of Hong Kong permanent residents. These children are given the right of abode by the Basic Law. The long queue of spouses and children who do not have the right of abode poses another challenge. This latter group has been waiting for years in the Mainland to immigrate to Hong Kong to be reunited with their Hong Kong resident family members.

After reunification with China, opportunities emerge for the government of the Hong Kong Special Administrative Region

(SAR) to take greater control over its immigration policy. The year 1997 was an opportune time to start reviewing the policy, to assess the challenges and opportunities it poses with regard to Chinese immigration, and to propose changes. To do so is the second objective of this book.

The historical account, theses and policy proposals of this book are developed and presented in the following chapters. In Chapter 2 we present a brief history of Chinese immigration in Hong Kong, starting from the colony's early years through World War II, and continuing through to the civil war in China and to the abolition of the reached-base policy in October 1980. The historical background is outlined as to highlight the immigrant origin of the Hong Kong community, the waves of illegal immigration that have descended upon Hong Kong, and the tightening of the immigration policy over time.

Chapter 3 surveys the issues of Chinese immigration that have emerged in the transition period following the signing in 1984 of the Sino-British Joint Declaration on the future of Hong Kong. The granting of the right of abode to Mainland-born children of Hong Kong permanent residents by the Basic Law has given rise to a number of issues. In Chapter 3 we highlight the conflict over whether to allow these children to immigrate to Hong Kong expeditiously or whether to adhere to the strict quotas at present. We assess the problems of the long queue of the long waiting period, and of child smuggling. We argue that the process of finding solutions to these problems is being stalled by lack of transparency and accountability, and afflicted by corruption of Chinese authorities responsible for the issuance of one-way permits. Arguments developed in the chapter are used to support proposed changes in the immigration policy in the final chapter. In Chapter 3 we also review several schemes for admitting Chinese professional and technical personnel from the Mainland and from overseas into Hong Kong to work, and we discuss the problems that may emerge.

Before proceeding to assess the contribution of immigration to Hong Kong's labour supply, we need to understand the background of immigrants, especially the recent ones. In Chapter 4 we review and analyze the characteristics of Chinese immigrants to show how earlier arrivals are different from recent arrivals. The earlier cohorts were predominantly made up of illegal male immigrants with little education. These cohorts had a high rate of participation in the labour force. Recent immigrants are, however, almost exclusively legal who are more likely to be women and children, because the criteria for selection have shifted towards family reunion. Recent cohorts are better educated but have a lower labour force participation rate than the earlier cohorts.

Immigration is a major source of population growth and of labour-force growth in Hong Kong. Hong Kong's fertility rate is one of the lowest in the world. The natural rate of increase in the population is below the replacement rate. Without an inflow of immigrants, the population of Hong Kong will shrink. Since 1995 each year immigration adds more people to the population of Hong Kong than does natural increase. Immigrants also add to the labour force. In the past, each wave of illegal immigration provided Hong Kong with a pool of unskilled labour. Halting the inflow of illegal immigrants beginning in 1980 was one of the main causes of Hong Kong's labour shortage from 1987 to 1994. An analysis of the contribution of immigration to population growth and to the labour supply appears in Chapter 5. This analysis lays the foundation for advocating in the final chapter a change in the immigration policy in support of population growth.

In Chapter 6 we dispel the fear that immigrants lower the wages of comparable native-born substantially, and that they displace native-born workers from jobs, one for one. We draw on theory and empirical studies to support the argument that immigration has little effect on wages and employment in the local labour market in the short run, except perhaps when there is a massive influx, and that it certainly has a negligible impact in the long run. We assess the contribution immigration has made to increasing the national income. We identify the groups that benefit from and those who are hurt by increased immigration. We also address the concern shared by many people that immigrants will become dependent on public assistance and that their consumption of public goods will cause congestion and impose a cost on society. We argue that in general increased immigration is primarily beneficial and that it has very little adverse impact overall on natives, provided that the eligibility requirements for public assistance and public housing are maintained or tightened.

The economic performance of immigrants in Hong Kong is analyzed in Chapter 7. We show that the average earnings of male immigrant employees are lower than those of natives and that the gap between the two widened between 1981 and 1996. Broadly speaking, early cohorts of immigrant employees have not been successful in assimilating into the Hong Kong economy. It was because of the widening differential over time in the rates of return to schooling and in the experience coefficient between natives and immigrants. It is argued that schooling and work experience acquired in the Mainland are less productive than those acquired in Hong Kong and that this becomes increasingly so as Hong Kong restructures into a service-oriented economy. This analysis provides the economic rationale for the ensuing proposal that immigrants should preferably be brought to Hong Kong when they are young so that they may complete part or most of their schooling in Hong Kong rather than finishing all of it in the Mainland.

Being relatively unsuccessful as employees, earlier immigrants turned to self-employment and entrepreneurship as an alternative. They were more likely to become employers and self-employed than natives were. Unlike their performance as employees, their performance as employers relative to that of natives has remained steady. Recent immigrant employers have, moreover, been very successful in closing the income gap with respect to native employers.

In Chapter 8 we address the concern that immigration may increase earnings inequality over time in Hong Kong. We show that in fact the reverse has occurred. The shift in the shares of natives and immigrants in the population accounts for about one-quarter of the increase in measured overall earnings inequality from 1981 to 1996. The cessation of the flow of illegal immigrants since 1980 has in fact inadvertently increased the measured earnings inequality.

Such a development has resulted from the more homogeneous (in earnings) new immigrants being replaced by the more heterogeneous (in earnings) natives and foreigners in population shares.

The book concludes with an assessment of the prevailing immigration policy and outlines proposals for policy change. It is argued that the immigration policy should be set to support long-term population growth at a target rate of 2% per annum rather than being framed merely in terms of controlling entry. The policy should be made transparent; its reformulation should include public consultation. The Hong Kong SAR government should negotiate with Beijing to recover control over who should be admitted as immigrants. The number to be admitted should be agreed upon with the Chinese government according to the Basic Law. The primary objective of the immigration policy should be to facilitate family reunion, and the secondary objective should be to supply skilled manpower for the economy.

A three-track immigration policy is proposed. First, Mainland-born children of Hong Kong permanent residents — children having right of abode under the Basic Law — and their immediate family members should be admitted to Hong Kong at any time they choose. There should be no quota restrictions. Other immigrants who do not have the right of abode should be admitted within the agreed-upon quota, with top priority being given to immediate family members of Hong Kong residents on the second track. The quota should be adjusted to enable spouses and children of Hong Kong residents to come to Hong Kong as soon as possible. On the third track, professional and technical personnel from the Mainland and overseas should be admitted outside the quota. The schemes and the numbers should be aligned to the changing economic demand in the labour market.

CHAPTER 2

A Brief History of Chinese Immigration in Hong Kong

Free Entry of Chinese Immigrants

Under the Peking Treaty signed by the Qing Dynasty and Britain in 1898, Chinese citizens could freely enter and leave Hong Kong. There was a free flow of residents between China and the New Territories, across the Chinese border. Most of the Chinese who entered Hong Kong in the early years were male workers who came to look for jobs. They usually left their families behind in the Mainland, and their families would join them in Hong Kong only after these men became established in the colony. This practice is reflected in the early population record of Hong Kong. Of the estimated total population of 23,817 in 1845, 19,201 were men, 2,862 were women, and 1,754 were children (Wong, 1997b).

In the early years, entry into Hong Kong from China was restricted only when there were outbreaks of contagious diseases. While non-Chinese residents were required to register in Hong Kong, people of Chinese descent were not. In 1923 the enactment of the Passport Ordinance required entrants into Hong Kong to possess valid passports or travel documents, but the Chinese were again exempt.

In any given year it was not uncommon for 10% to 20% of Hong Kong's population to return to China. This free flow of residents of Chinese descent across the border is best exemplified by the massive movement of population during and immediately after World War II. During the war a massive number of Chinese civilians fled from Hong Kong into China to escape Japanese occupation. Following the Japanese surrender, Chinese civilians returned at the rate of almost 100,000 a month. The population, which by August 1945 had been reduced to about 600,000, rose by the end of 1947 to an estimated 1.8 million.

Controlling Chinese Immigration

In the period 1948–49, as the forces of the Chinese Nationalist government began to face defeat in the civil war at the hands of the Communists, immigrants from China flowed into Hong Kong at a rate unparalleled in Hong Kong's history. Hundreds of thousands of refugees entered the territory during 1949 and the spring of 1950. Although most of them were farmers and labourers from Guangdong, a significant number were industrialists and entrepreneurs from Shanghai who brought with them capital, managerial skills, and technical know-how. The latter group made an important contribution to the early industrialization of Hong Kong in the 1950s. In 1950 the balance of arrivals over departures in Hong Kong reached an all-time high of 339,689 (see Table 2.1). By mid-1950 the population was estimated to be 2.5 million.[1]

For a short time following the change of government in China in 1949, Chinese citizens were still free to enter Hong Kong. Chinese citizens who held passes issued by the Chinese authorities were allowed to enter Hong Kong either for short-term visits or for establishing residence. However, the large inflow of Chinese citizens coming into Hong Kong to escape communist rule soon made the policy of unrestricted entry untenable. In May 1950 the Hong Kong government implemented a quota system to restrict the entry of Chinese citizens. The quota initially applied only to entrants from Taiwan and other parts of China. Entrants from Guangdong were exempt.

The new Chinese government protested the restriction of entry into Hong Kong by quota. It refused to recognize the three treaties that ceded Hong Kong and leased the New Territories. It maintained that since Hong Kong was part of China, Chinese citizens had freedom of movement within Chinese territories and that Britain had no right to restrict such movement. After negotiation, the Chinese and British governments reached an agreement. The Chinese government would decide on the number of entrants to be allowed to enter Hong Kong from China and would vet and approve the applications for entry into Hong Kong. The Hong Kong government would accept all Chinese citizens who had been issued exit permits by the Chinese government for entry into Hong Kong for residence. However, in recognition of Hong Kong's population pressure, the Chinese government would restrict the number of people granted exit permits, holders of the so-called "one-way permit". With the exception of two brief periods of suspension in 1955 and 1956, this quota system has continued until today.

Discretion on Illegal Immigrants and the Reached-Base Policy

After the agreement was reached, the stream of Chinese immigrants flowing to Hong Kong has been rather steady. The net balance of departures and arrivals in Hong Kong averaged about 50,000 to 60,000 per year from 1952 to 1956. The stream of immigrants from China tapered off after 1954, as China tightened the exit of its citizens. Although the exact numbers of Chinese immigrants into Hong Kong are not available, the dwindling stream is reflected in the decline in the balance of departures over arrivals, from about 62,000 in 1954 to about 28,000 in 1959 (see Table 2.1).

Until the 1950s, immigrants from China came to Hong Kong mostly for reuniting with their families or for political reasons. In the early 1950s Hong Kong's economy was still backward. An unskilled worker in Hong Kong probably would not fare much better in terms of standard of living than he would in China. The situation changed in 1958. In China the Great Leap Forward and the collectivization movement in agriculture led to widespread starvation. An estimated 27 million people died during the movement (Lin, 1990). According to one estimate, grain output was down by 15% in 1959, by another 16% in 1960, and did not return to 1952

Table 2.1

Population Growth and Balance of Arrivals and Departures, 1948–96

Year	Estimated Population (mid-year)	Balance of Arrivals and Departures*	Legal Immigrants from China
1948	1,800,000	18,358	n.a.
1949	1,857,000	20,736	n.a.
1950	2,237,000	339,689	n.a.
1951	2,015,000	−267,028	n.a.
1952	2,126,000	59,781	n.a.
1953	2,242,000	61,119	n.a.
1954	2,365,000	62,361	n.a.
1955	2,490,000	57,267	n.a.
1956	2,615,000	50,559	n.a.
1957	2,736,000	43,040	n.a.
1958	2,854,000	35,730	n.a.
1959	2,967,000	27,801	n.a.
1960	3,075,000	70,075	n.a.
1961	3,168,100	−15,374[#]	n.a.
1962	3,305,200	81,260	n.a.
1963	3,420,900	−558	n.a.
1964	3,504,600	−5,737	n.a.
1965	3,597,900	−2,638	n.a.
1966	3,629,900	−18,638	n.a.
1967	3,722,800	13,271	n.a.
1968	3,802,700	20,598	n.a.
1969	3,863,900	−1,602	n.a.
1970	3,959,000	30,151	n.a.
1971	4,045,300	40,701	n.a.
1972	4,123,600	29,787	n.a.
1973	4,241,600	88,977	n.a.
1974	4,377,800	42,619	n.a.
1975	4,461,600	4,043	n.a.
1976	4,518,000	−5,711	n.a.
1977	4,583,700	23,809	n.a.
1978	4,667,500	76,117	n.a.
1979	4,870,500	147,388	n.a.
1980	5,024,400	91,708	55,452
1981	5,163,100	39,422	54,249
1982	5,253,200	23,683	53,848
1983	5,332,000	990	26,701
1984	5,385,300	2,690	27,475
1985	5,445,400	20,991	27,285
1986	5,516,300	21,059	27,111
1987	5,572,400	4,859	27,268
1988	5,609,800	− 8,389	28,137
1989	5,638,500	−15,540	27,263
1990	5,649,800	−9,072	27,976
1991	5,690,800	15,613	26,782
1992	5,746,800	46,621	28,367
1993	5,860,200	83,883	32,909
1994	6,007,900	86,874	38,218
1995	6,133,000	116,322	45,986
1996	6,293,000	132,935	61,179

Source: *Hong Kong Statistics*, 1947–67, Demographic Statistics Section, Census and Statistics Department, Immigration Department (February 1995).

Note: All numbers exclude Vietnamese boat people. n.a. = data not available.
*End year comparison. For 1986–96, the figures include an estimate of Hong Kong residents away to China / Macau living outside Hong Kong.
[#]From 7 March 1961 to 31 December 1961.

levels until 1962. A rapid surge in illegal immigration from China resulted. These immigrants were illegal in that they did not have exit permits issued by the Chinese authorities. The Immigration Department of Hong Kong exercised discretion in allowing these illegal immigrants to register and stay in Hong Kong. This was the first wave of illegal immigration from China into Hong Kong since the imposition of immigration control by quota in 1950. It was reported that as many as 142,000 refugees crossed the border illegally into Hong Kong from 1959 to 1962. By 1961 as much as 50.5% of Hong Kong's population were born in China. (Table 2.2)

Table 2.2
Place of Birth of Population, 1961–86
(%)

Place of Birth	Year					
	1961	1966	1971	1976	1981	1986
Hong Kong	47.7	53.8	56.4	58.9	57.2	59.3
China	50.5	n.a.	41.6	38.6	39.6	37.1
Elsewhere	1.8	n.a.	2.0	2.5	3.2	3.6
Total	100.0	100.0	100.0	100.0	100.0	100.0

Source: Hong Kong Census 1961 and 1971, and Hong Kong By-Census, 1966, 1976 and 1986. n.a. = Breakdown not available.

By 1963 the economic situation in China had stabilized and an economic recovery was under way. Immigration into Hong Kong continued, but at a much slower pace. The period from the end of the Great Leap Forward by 1963 to 1969 is unique as far as migration is concerned. With the exception of 1967 and 1968, the balance of arrivals into and departures out of Hong Kong was negative. The flow of legal immigrants into Hong Kong was small during this period, especially after the beginning of the Cultural Revolution in 1966, when it became difficult to obtain exit permits to go to Hong Kong.

The small flow of legal immigrants was more than offset by a wave of emigration from Hong Kong during the late 1960s. This

Table 2.3
Illegal Immigration from China, 1970–95

Year	Arrests Upon Entry Annual (per day)		Evaders[1] Annual (per day)		Total Annual (per day)	
1970	3,416	(9.4)	3,416	(9.4)		
1971	5,062	(13.9)	5,062	(13.9)		
1972	12,958	(35.5)	12,958	(35.5)		
1973	17,561	(48.1)	17,561	(48.1)		
1974[2]	235	(0.6)	19,565	(53.6)	19,800	(54.3)
1975	1,150	(3.2)	7,100	(19.5)	8,250	(22.6)
1976	828	(2.3)	7,226	(19.8)	8,054	(22.1)
1977	1,815	(5.0)	6,546	(17.9)	8,361	(22.9)
1978	8,205	(22.5)	11,233	(30.8)	19,438	(53.3)
1979	89,940	(246.4)	102,826	(281.7)	192,766	(528.1)
1980[3]	82,125	(225.0)	67,964	(186.2)	150,089	(411.2)
1981	7,530	(20.7)	1,690	(4.6)	9,220	(25.3)
1982	8,676	(23.8)	2,484	(6.8)	11,160	(30.6)
1983	4,671	(12.8)	2,933	(8.0)	7,604	(20.8)
1984	9,653	(26.5)	3,090	(8.5)	12,743	(34.9)
1985	12,616	(34.6)	3,394	(9.3)	16,010	(43.9)
1986	16,832	(46.1)	3,707	(10.2)	20,539	(56.3)
1987	22,425	(61.4)	4,282	(11.7)	26,707	(73.2)
1988	13,581	(37.1)	7,227	(19.7)	20,808	(56.9)
1989	5,452	(14.9)	10,389	(28.5)	15,841	(43.4)
1990	9,592	(26.3)	18,234	(50.0)	27,826	(76.2)
1991	n.a.		n.a.		25,422	(69.6)
1992	n.a.		n.a.		35,645	(97.7)
1993	n.a.		n.a.		37,517	(102.8)
1994	n.a.		n.a.		31,521	(86.4)
1995	n.a.		n.a.		26,824	(73.5)

Source: Immigration Department.

Note: [1] Evaders are illegal immigrants caught beyond the first net of apprehension. Prior to 1974 no distinction between evaders and those arrested upon entry was made. Prior to October 1980 evaders were permitted to stay in Hong Kong.

         [2] Implementation of the reached-base policy.

         [3] Ending of the reached-base policy in October.

         Brackets indicate average number per day.

wave was to continue until the early 1970s, when many overseas receiving countries drastically curtailed immigration. Emigrants from Hong Kong in this period were mainly those who had lost confidence in Hong Kong because of political campaigns in China and social instability and riots in Hong Kong. These individuals — for example restaurant workers from the New Territories who mostly settled in Britain and students going abroad to study who did not return — sought a better standard of living overseas. The positive balance of arrivals and departures in 1967 and 1968 was due to a surge of illegal immigration into Hong Kong at the height of political turmoils in the early years of the Cultural Revolution in China.

Throughout the two decades from 1950 to the mid-1970s, Hong Kong and Guangdong were rather segregated from each other in terms of transport links. The common modes of illegal entry were by boat, by swimming, or by crossing the fenced border. Even when the flow of illegal immigrants was sizeable then, the Hong Kong government exercised discretion and allowed these illegal immigrants to stay in Hong Kong, whether or not they had been apprehended by the police. However, toward the end of this period, the flow of illegal immigrants began to increase dramatically. In 1970 an average of 9.4 illegal immigrants were caught every day, but by 1974 this number had increased to 54.3 (see Table 2.3). This prompted the Hong Kong government to become stricter about granting residence status to illegal immigrants.

In 1974 the Hong Kong government discontinued the practice of allowing all immigrants from China to remain in Hong Kong and replaced it with what came to be known as the reached-base policy. Under this new policy those arrested on illegal arrival in Hong Kong were repatriated to China. However, all those who evaded capture and subsequently "reached base" were permitted to stay in Hong Kong. Reaching base means crossing the border without being captured and establishing a home with relatives or finding accommodation.

The reached-base policy in relation to illegal immigration is a policy that sits halfway between allowing all illegal immigrants to stay in Hong Kong and prohibiting them from obtaining residence status. The Hong Kong government was reluctant to remove those illegal immigrants who were established in Hong Kong. There was a fear that if the police continued to track them down and capture them after they had entered the urban areas, they would be forced to go underground. An illegal community would then form, which would resort to illegal means of making a living and which would be vulnerable to the exploitation of unscrupulous employers.

Abolition of the Reached-Base Policy

During the first three years after the implementation of the reached-base policy, about 7,000 illegal immigrants from China reached base every year (see Table 2.3, 1975–77). The number of illegal immigrants permitted to stay in Hong Kong was half that before the policy was implemented. This number could be absorbed into the Hong Kong community without much strain. The temporary equilibrium was, however, rather fragile. Any change in economic or political circumstances in China would upset the balance, and this happened in 1978.

In late 1978 China launched its economic reform and open-door policy. The barrier that had hitherto effectively inhibited the flow of capital, people, and information between China and the outside world in three decades of isolation under communist rule was essentially removed. Isolationism during the Cultural Revolution (1966–76) had been particularly repressive. Any form of contact or linkage with friends or relatives outside China was considered reactionary and could result in political purging. It was at the end of this era of repressive isolationism that China opened up under the leadership of Deng Xiaoping. Suddenly people in China, especially those in the rural communes, became aware for the first time of the outside world through access to information and contact with travellers. They became especially aware of the vast difference in the standard and style of living of people in China and those in Hong Kong.

Under the open-door policy, social and political control in China at the local level eroded. It became much easier for peasants from communes to travel and to reach the Hong Kong border. The consequence was dramatic. Hong Kong was bombarded by an onslaught of illegal immigration that was in every way more massive than the previous wave that had entered the territory during the Great Leap Forward in 1962.

This wave of illegal immigration gathered momentum and increased in strength from 1978 to 1980. The average daily number of illegal immigrants arrested at the Hong Kong border increased over ten times, from about 23 in 1978 to 246 in 1979 (see Table 2.3). The daily number that evaded capture and reached base increased from 31 to 282 in the same period. On the other side of the border, the Chinese authorities also used all means, including exhortation, punishment, and border patrols to try to stem the flood. It was estimated that for every three would-be illegal immigrants apprehended by the Chinese security forces at the border, two slipped past the border into Hong Kong.

The situation was aggravated by the concurrent arrival of immigrants with legal exit permits issued by the Chinese authorities to visit Hong Kong or to stop there in transit to other countries. In 1980 about 55,452 people in total, or 152 per day, arrived in Hong Kong, and most remained permanently.

The massive inflow of immigrants, illegal as well as legal, caused disruption in and distortion of Hong Kong's social and physical infrastructure. Throughout the 1970s the Hong Kong government had been planning for the expansion of social services and infrastructure in schools, hospitals, housing, public transport, and welfare facilities on the assumption that the population would grow at a rate of 2% per annum. The massive wave of illegal immigration from 1978 to 1980 caused the population growth rate to accelerate at a rate of 5% per annum, putting unbearable pressure on the infrastructure.

The massive inflow of illegal immigrants also had an adverse impact on wages and employment in Hong Kong. The addition of over 300,000 largely unskilled immigrants to the labour market from 1978 to 1980 depressed real wages. The situation was aggravated by the slowdown of the Hong Kong economy from 1981 to 1982.

The situation became untenable in August and September of 1980, when in each of the two months an estimated 23,000 illegal immigrants — nearly half of whom evaded arrest and reached base — arrived in Hong Kong. The Hong Kong government, after informing and seeking the co-operation of the Chinese authorities, announced the abolition of the reached-base policy on 23 October 1980. Illegal immigrants who were already in Hong Kong were allowed three days to register for an official identity card. After this grace period, all illegal immigrants would be repatriated to China immediately after capture regardless of whether they had reached base or not. The door to legal residence in Hong Kong for illegal immigrants was finally closed.

To buttress the abolition of the reached-base policy, legislation was enacted to require all adult residents of Hong Kong to carry identity cards or some other acceptable proof of identity at all times. The police were empowered to demand that suspected illegal immigrants produce their identity cards when stopped in the street. Employers were also required to inspect identity cards of all those they recruited and employed. It became a criminal offence to employ individuals with no identity cards. Furthermore, proof of identity was required of individuals seeking public government services.

Following the abolition of the reached-base policy, the tide of illegal immigrants subsided to a more manageable level in the early 1980s. Since the abolition, the flow of entrants who eventually took up residence in Hong Kong was dominated by legal immigrants from China. Increasingly, the composition of this flow was biased towards family reunion.

In October 1980, after the reached-base policy had been abolished, the Hong Kong government and the Chinese government agreed to restrict to 150 a day the issuance of one-way permits that allowed holders to enter Hong Kong to take up residence. This was down from a peak of 310 in December 1978. This daily quota of one-way permits was subsequently revised downward to 75 in 1983 and remained at that level for ten years until 1993.

During this period, besides one-way permits, the Chinese authorities issued an unlimited number of two-way permits, which allow holders to visit Hong Kong for the purpose of visiting family or doing business. Holders must return to China after a designated period. However, many overstayed their visits and applied for permanent residence in Hong Kong. The Hong Kong government changed the regulation and ceased granting residence status to Chinese entrants holding two-way permits. Following this change in regulation, only holders of one-way permits from China were granted residence in Hong Kong. However, the overstaying of two-way permit holders from China continues to be a problem. For instance, in 1991 as many as 22,566, or 5% of the two-way permit holders from China, overstayed (Kwong, 1993). The number increased to 27,250 in 1994 (Skeldon, 1995). The government responded to the problem by imposing a fine of HK$5,000 and a two-year prison term on overstayers. With the closing of the door on two-way permit holders, the only way for Mainland residents to gain residence status in Hong Kong is by way of legal entry through obtaining a one-way permit issued in China.

Note

1. For an account of Chinese immigration after 1949, see Ho, Lam, and Liu (1991).

CHAPTER 3

Current Issues of Chinese Immigration in Hong Kong

Right of Abode

Following the signing of the Sino-British Joint Declaration on the future of Hong Kong in 1984, the Hong Kong government amended the Immigration Ordinance in 1987. The amendment provides for the "right of abode" to include the right to land, the right of unconditional stay in Hong Kong, and the right to not to be deported out of Hong Kong. It also defines "Hong Kong permanent resident" as a person who enjoys these rights. Permanent residents are:

1. Citizens of British Dependent Territories,
2. Chinese citizens who ordinarily reside in Hong Kong for not less than seven years, or
3. Citizens of the British Commonwealth who obtained the right to land in Hong Kong before 1983.

The Registration of Persons Ordinance was also amended to provide for the issuance of "permanent identity cards" to persons defined as Hong Kong permanent residents, and the issuance of "ordinary identity cards" to other people in Hong Kong. The amendment of these ordinances prepared Hong Kong for the transition to take place in 1997.

In April 1990 the Basic Law was passed. Its Article 24 specifies that permanent residents of the Hong Kong Special Administrative Region (SAR) shall have the right of abode in Hong Kong. The Basic

Table 3.1

Hong Kong Residents with Spouses in China by Age Group of Residents, 1991

Age of Residents	Number of Residents	Percent
20–29	5,500	5.8
30–39	27,400	28.8
40–49	22,300	23.4
50–59	19,700	20.7
60 and above	20,300	21.3
Total	95,200	100.0

Source: Census and Statistics Department, General Household Survey, *Hong Kong Residents Married in China, 1991.*

Law defines permanent residents as being persons under one of the following six categories:

1. Chinese citizens born in Hong Kong before or after the establishment of the Hong Kong Special Administrative Region,

2. Chinese citizens who have ordinarily resided in Hong Kong for a continuous period of not less than seven years before or after the establishment of the Hong Kong Special Administrative Region,

3. Persons of Chinese nationality born outside Hong Kong of those residents listed in categories (1) and (2),

4. Persons not of Chinese nationality who have entered Hong Kong with valid travel documents, who have ordinarily resided in Hong Kong for a continuous period of not less than seven years, and who have taken Hong Kong as their place of permanent residence before or after the establishment of the Hong Kong Special Administrative Region,

5. Persons under twenty-one years of age born in Hong Kong of those residents listed in category (4) before or after the establishment of the Hong Kong Special Administrative Region, or

6. Persons other than those residents listed in categories (1) to (5), who, before the establishment of the Hong Kong

Special Administrative Region, had the right of abode in Hong Kong only.

When the Basic Law was passed in 1990, it was not fully appreciated that the category (3) provision for permanent residents would cause serious legal as well as practical problems for the Hong Kong SAR Government after 1 July 1997.

Immigration and Family Reunion

Since Hong Kong has for long been a society of immigrants, many Hong Kong residents have family ties in China. A 1991 General Household Survey on Hong Kong residents estimated that 95,200 Hong Kong residents had married spouses who were still living in China as of the second quarter of 1991. Some 93% of these Hong Kong residents were men. Most were older persons who had come to Hong Kong many years ago. Over 40% were fifty years of age or older. Some 37% were married before 1971. Their age distribution is shown in Table 3.1.

These Hong Kong residents had a total of 310,200 children living in China whose age distribution is shown in Table 3.2. Most of these children were adults, with 40% being thirty years of age or older. Less than 30% were children of age below fifteen. These estimated 310,200 children of Hong Kong residents living in China are a pool of individuals who potentially would have the right of abode in Hong Kong after 1997. According to Article 24 of the Basic Law, children of permanent residents of Hong Kong born outside Hong Kong (in this case in the Mainland) are entitled to the right of abode. The Preparatory Committee of the Hong Kong Special Administrative Region has interpreted this Article to mean that only a child whose mother or father was a permanent resident of Hong Kong at the time of that child's birth would have the right of abode. This interpretation will reduce the pool of children eligible for the right of abode in Hong Kong to below 310,200. Nevertheless, the pool could still be quite large.

The size of this pool of children and the fear that all those eligible would rush into Hong Kong at once after 1 July 1997, when

Table 3.2

Children of Hong Kong Residents Residing in China by Age, 1991

Age of Children	Number of Children	Percent
Under 5	32,300	10.4
5– 9	30,600	9.9
10–14	27,800	9.0
15–19	33,800	10.9
20–29	56,300	18.1
30–39	50,300	16.2
40–49	50,500	16.3
50 and above	28,500	9.2
Total	310,200	100.0

Source: Census and Statistics Department, General Household Survey, *Hong Kong Residents Married in China, 1991*.

the Basic Law takes effect, prompted the Hong Kong government to negotiate with the Chinese government to increase the daily entry quota to let in more children orderly. The two governments agreed to increase the daily entry quota from 75 to 105 in November 1993. The additional 30 people per day were to be the spouses and children of Hong Kong permanent residents. Fifteen of these were to be children. It was estimated that in the first five years after the quota increased, social spending on education, health, housing, and transportation in Hong Kong would have to be increased by $400 million and administrative spending by $100 million.

Shortly after this increase was implemented, the two governments agreed to increase the daily entry quota of one-way permit holders further to 150. This increase went into effect on 1 July 1995. Of the additional 45 people allowed into Hong Kong each day, 15 were to be spouses of Hong Kong permanent residents and 30 were to be their children below the age of twenty. In the first year following the increase, among the 30 spots allocated to children, 15 were to be allocated to the 0–5 age group, and the rest were to be allocated to the 16–20 age group. Children in the 6–15 age group were not to be allocated any of the increased spots in the first year of implementation. Their allocation was postponed for one year to phase in with the downward trend in school enrolment that began in 1995–96.

The granting of the right of abode to Chinese citizens born in Hong Kong under category (1), and to children of Hong Kong permanent residents under category (3), induced new waves of illegal immigrants who were different from those that made up the previous waves. Pregnant mothers from China entered Hong Kong illegally (or overstayed after gaining entry with two-way permits) to give birth to children in hospitals in Hong Kong. Their parents tried to gain residence status for the babies. Under the regulation in place until 1 July 1997 the children were to gain residence status only if their fathers have residence status. The new-born children were to be permitted to stay in Hong Kong, but their mothers were to be repatriated. If their fathers were in China, both the new-born children and the mothers must be repatriated. It was reported that there were 1,746 such births of children who were permitted to stay in Hong Kong in 1990, 2,750 in 1991, and 9,000 in 1994 (Kwong, 1993; Skeldon, 1995). It was estimated that these births accounted for as much as 12% of the total number of births in Hong Kong for 1994.

Another category of illegal immigrants induced to enter Hong Kong is that of Mainland-born children of Hong Kong parents. The smuggling of children into Hong Kong reached a peak during 1986–87. From October 1986 to March 1987 a total of 220 young illegal immigrants were arrested upon entry, and another 732 who had evaded arrest emerged (*Hong Kong Annual Report*, 1988, pp. 304–305). Smugglers, popularly known as "snake heads", took advantage of the Immigration Department's humanitarian policy of allowing a few illegal children immigrants to stay in Hong Kong by inciting parents to pay a hefty fee to arrange for the smuggling of their children into Hong Kong. There were reports of children being drowned or deserted during their journey to Hong Kong when the smugglers were pursued by the police. The policy was tightened in April 1987, and the situation was brought under control for the time being.

Table 3.3

**Application for One-way Permits for Children
(of Hong Kong Residents)
Living in Guangdong up to 15 July 1997**

Applications received in Guangdong Province	130,000
Applications sent to Hong Kong government for review	104,359
Applications returned by Hong Kong to Guangdong	91,301
(a) Disqualified	1,319
(b) Pending further information	22,068
(c) Qualified	67,914
(i) Already arrived in Hong Kong	36,004
(ii) Waiting for one-way permits	31,910

Source: *Sing Tao Daily*, 16 July 1997

The smuggling of young children into Hong Kong picked up again in 1997, just months before the changeover of sovereignty. Parents who are Hong Kong residents were once again induced by rumours of amnesty to arrange for the smuggling of their young children from the Mainland into Hong Kong. Some of these illegal immigrants were as young as six years old. This time the parents hoped that if their children could remain in Hong Kong beyond 1 July 1997 without being detected or repatriated, they would be entitled to the right of abode under Article 24 of the Basic Law, which was to take effect on that date.

The Hong Kong government responded by taking a tough stand on a few very visible cases that were widely covered in the media. In one case that attracted the most attention, the child concerned had been smuggled into Hong Kong six years earlier and had been residing in Hong Kong since. The government, in the public eye, repatriated this child as well as others. It also sought the co-operation of the Chinese government to crack down on the snake heads, and to reduce the uncertainty of the long wait of applicants for one-way permits to Hong Kong by making the approval process more transparent.

Child Immigrants After 1 July 1997

The issue of the immigration of Mainland-born children of Hong Kong permanent residents heated up again after 1 July 1997. According to Article 24 of the Basic Law, these children have the right of abode in Hong Kong after 1 July 1997, and the right of abode guarantees that they cannot be deported. Therefore, these children could, theoretically, have all entered Hong Kong after 1 July with or without one-way permits issued by the Chinese authorities and they could have demanded their right of abode.

The Hong Kong government's Immigration Department initially estimated that there were about 35,000 children of Hong Kong permanent residents born in China waiting to immigrate to Hong Kong after 1 July 1997. This number was subsequently revised upward. In July 1997 a new estimate of 66,000 children was announced, of whom about 60% are between the age of six and fifteen. Not much information has been released by the Hong Kong SAR government on how it arrived at this estimate. However, available figures such as those shown in Table 3.2 would suggest that the figure is likely to be an underestimate. Figures released by the Public Security Bureau of Guangdong Province (neighbouring Hong Kong) shed some light on the magnitude of the problem.

Table 3.3 shows that the number of applications for one-way permits by children in Guangdong born of Hong Kong parents was about 130,000 in July 1997, of which 104,359 cases were sent by Guangdong to Hong Kong for review. Of the latter only 1,319 were disqualified, and among the 22,068 cases that require further information, probably most will qualify eventually. Waiting in the queue are another 31,910 cases that have already been approved for the issue of one-way permits for entry into Hong Kong. Meanwhile, there are still another 30,000 cases or more not shown in Table 3.3 that are being processed by the authorities in Guangdong, and the great majority of these cases are likely to qualify also. Hence, in Guangdong Province alone, the number of children eligible for the right of abode in Hong Kong could well exceed 66,000. On the basis of a daily quota of 42 assigned to Guangdong for children, Public Security Bureau of Guangdong officials have estimated that it would take about six and a half years to send all those eligible to Hong Kong.

In the agreement reached with the Chinese authorities in 1993, 15 spots in the daily quota of 105 were designated for children. The daily quota was raised to 150 in 1995, and the designated quota for children increased to 45. The Hong Kong government in fact further requested that a floating daily quota of 21 out of the remaining undesignated quota be allocated to eligible children, bringing the total up to 66. Apparently, though, there was no commitment on the part of the Chinese authorities. In actual fact, in 1994 a daily average of only 9.3 children arrived in Hong Kong, when the daily quota should have been 15. In 1996 an average of 55.4 children arrived, when the designated quota was 45 and the combined designated and floating quota was 66 (*Ming Pao*, 17 July 1997). It has been reported that the Immigration Department of the Hong Kong SAR government is negotiating with the Beijing authorities to increase the daily quota designated for eligible children to 90, with the aim of allowing the estimated 66,000 eligible children to enter Hong Kong within two years after 1 July 1997.

In the meantime Guangdong Province authorities have increased the daily quota for one-way permits for children of Hong Kong permanent residents to 60 with effect from 1 January 1998. Starting from October 1997, adult sons and daughters aged 20 or above of Hong Kong permanent residents were also allowed to apply for one-way permits in Guangdong. Since there has been no published estimate of this number, it is difficult to estimate how these two measures will affect the waiting time for one way-permits.

While the Hong Kong SAR government was planning for the orderly entry into Hong Kong of children eligible for the right of abode under Article 24 of the Basic Law, the issue of visas to child immigrants took a sharp turn after 1 July 1997. Within the first three working days after the establishment of the Hong Kong SAR, 380 children who had entered Hong Kong illegally, mostly before 1

July 1997, surfaced and registered with their parents in Hong Kong at the Immigration Department, demanding their right of abode.

The Hong Kong SAR government emphasized the importance of the orderly entry of children eligible for the right of abode within a planned time schedule. It was concerned that any relaxation of the administrative control of entry would invite an avalanche of arrivals of eligible children still residing in China. The pressure put on the social infrastructure would be too great if all the eligible children were admitted within a short period. For instance, it was estimated that to provide schooling for all the school-age children who made up about 60% of the estimated 66,000 children eligible for the right of abode, sixteen schools would have to be built.

The Hong Kong SAR government reacted hastily to the surge of child immigrants who registered with the Immigration Department within a few days after 1 July 1997. An Immigration Amendment Bill with three motions for debate was pushed through the Provisional Legislative Council in one day on 10 July 1997. This bill, which took retroactive effect on 1 July 1997, requires children who are eligible for the right of abode under Article 24 of the Basic Law to file their applications in the Mainland to have their eligibility assessed there first. Cases that pass the first assessment in the Mainland will be sent to Hong Kong for further checking. Those who qualify will be issued a certificate of entitlement of the right of abode, which the Hong Kong SAR government will send to the Chinese authorities. This certificate together with the one-way permit issued by the Chinese authorities will enable eligible children to enter Hong Kong. The crucial administrative procedure is that applications for the certificate of entitlement of the right of abode will not be accepted in Hong Kong and must be filed in the Mainland (or overseas). This means that children already in Hong Kong who may well have the right of abode under Article 24 of the Basic Law will be repatriated to the Mainland, where they will have to file their applications.

This bill was immediately challenged by members of the legal profession. As many as 100 members of the Hong Kong Bar Association and the Law Society of Hong Kong volunteered legal

Table 3.4

Provincial Origin of Legal Immigrants from China, 1991–96

Province	Year					
	1991	1992	1993	1994	1995	1996
Guangdong	12,467	12,466	16,597	19,804	29,381	43,532
	(46.5)	(43.9)	(50.4)	(51.8)	(63.9)	(71.2)
Fujian	7,260	8,425	9,135	10,716	8,758	9,565
	(27.1)	(29.7)	(27.8)	(28.0)	(19.0)	(15.6)
Hainan	936	807	995	988	1,074	1,147
	(3.5)	(2.8)	(3.0)	(2.6)	(2.3)	(1.9)
Shanghai	1,016	1,076	990	1,018	1,229	1,129
	(3.8)	(3.8)	(3.0)	(2.7)	(2.7)	(1.8)
Others	4,958	5,555	5,192	5,692	5,544	5,806
	(18.5)	(19.6)	(15.8)	(14.9)	(12.1)	(9.5)
Unknown	143	37	0	0	0	0
	(0.5)	(0.1)	(0)	(0)	(0)	(0)
Total	26,782	28,366	32,909	38,218	45,986	61,179

Source: Census and Statistics Department.
Note: Column percentages in brackets.

assistance to families of these eligible children already in Hong Kong to seek judicial review on the grounds that the imposition of administrative hurdles infringes on the right of these children, which they automatically possessed on 1 July 1997 when the Basic Law took effect. These lawyers argued that the bill passed by the Provisional Legislative Council violates the Basic Law. A court injunction that stopped the Immigration Department from repatriating these children pending judicial review was issued. Litigation on their cases and the many to follow will take some time to conclude. The Court of First Instance ruled in favour of the government, but it is likely that the legal battle will ultimately have to be settled in the Court of Final Appeal.

On 26 January 1998, the High Court also ruled that Mainland-born sons and daughters of Hong Kong residents are entitled to the right of abode in Hong Kong even though their parents were not permanent residents of Hong Kong at the time of their birth. According to the Basic Law, they are entitled to the right of abode in

Hong Kong once their parents gained permanent residence status. This interpretation of the Basic Law will effectively increase the pool eligible for the right of abode to over 310,000 (see Table 3.2). The SAR Government will appeal against this decision.

Approval of One-Way Permits by the Chinese Government

Following the signing of the Sino-British Joint Declaration on Hong Kong in 1984, the Chinese government issued a set of regulations governing Chinese citizens immigrating to Hong Kong and Macau to settle. The following categories of applicants are eligible to apply:

1. Applicants whose spouses are residing in Hong Kong or Macau and who have been separated for many years,
2. Applicants who have old or sick parents residing in Hong Kong or Macau who need their care,
3. Old people and children who have no one to support them in China may apply to go to Hong Kong or Macau to be under the care of their relatives there,
4. Applicants who are the sole inheritors of estates of deceased relatives in Hong Kong or Macau, or
5. Other applicants with special considerations.

Applicants must apply to the Public Security Bureau of their place of residence in the Mainland. Successful applicants will be issued a "Permit for Proceeding to Hong Kong and Macau", more commonly known as the one-way exit permit.

The agreed-upon quota of one-way permits is divided among the provinces, with the largest number being allocated to Guangdong. Table 3.4 shows that the percentage of legal immigrants from Guangdong to Hong Kong increased substantially, from 46.5% of the total in 1991 to 71.2% in 1996. Without further information on the way quotas are divided among the provinces, it is difficult to assess the reason for this large increase in quotas for Guangdong from 1991 to 1996. One possible interpretation is that the pressure for allocating more quotas for family reunion has built up

Table 3.5
Waiting Period of Legal Immigrants from China
who Entered Hong Kong in 1995 and 1996

Length of Waiting	1995		1996	
(years of waiting)	Persons	%	Persons	%
< 1	7,906	(17.20)	8,829	(14.400)
1– 2	14,999	(32.60)	21,478	(35.000)
2– 3	6,295	(13.70)	13,088	(21.400)
3– 4	6,431	(14.00)	8,888	(14.500)
4– 5	2,385	(5.20)	3,248	(5.300)
5– 6	2,696	(5.90)	1,221	(2.000)
6– 7	1,116	(2.40)	1,298	(2.100)
7– 8	773	(1.70)	568	(0.900)
8– 9	700	(1.50)	529	(0.900)
9–10	653	(1.40)	344	(0.600)
10–11	751	(1.60)	450	(0.700)
11–12	925	(2.00)	804	(1.300)
15–20	279	(0.60)	349	(0.500)
20–25	57	(0.10)	64	(0.100)
>25	12	(0.03)	20	(0.030)
Unknown	8	(0.02)	1	(0.001)
Total	45,986	(100)	61,179	(100)

Source: Security Branch, Hong Kong government. *Ming Pao*, 24 April 1997.

tremendously in the last few years, and the central government is obliged to reallocate more quotas from other provinces to Guangdong, where the great majority of the spouses and children of Hong Kong residents live.

The implementation of these regulations by Chinese authorities is fraught with problems. There is neither transparency in the processing of applications nor consistency in applying the above criteria in issuing one-way permits across provincial authorities or within the same issuing authority. Corruption has been widely reported. It has been alleged that bribes in the amount of 100,000 renminbi (HK$94,000) have had to be paid to secure one-way permits for those who are ineligible to apply, or to speed up the approval of eligible applicants.

Table 3.6

**Legal Immigrants from China who Entered Hong Kong
by Type of Relatives in Hong Kong, 1991–96**

Types of Relatives in Hong Kong	1991	1992	1993	1994	1995	1996
Only have parent (s) in Hong Kong	12,798 (47.8)	13,116 (46.2)	15,699 (47.7)	18,241 (47.7)	22,529 (49.0)	31,715 (51.8)
Only have spouse in Hong Kong	10,513 (39.3)	10,906 (38.4)	13,060 (39.7)	16,129 (42.2)	12,858 (28.0)	17,165 (28.1)
Only have child (ren) in Hong Kong	703 (2.6)	806 (2.8)	926 (2.8)	798 (2.1)	685 (1.5)	634 (1.0)
Have a combination of parent(s) and / or spouse and / or child (ren) in Hong Kong	238 (0.9)	424 (1.5)	528 (1.6)	473 (1.2)	7,214 (15.7)	9,323 (15.2)
Have no next-of-kin in Hong Kong	2,530 (9.4)	3,114 (11.0)	2,696 (8.2)	2,577 (6.7)	2,700 (5.9)	2,342 (3.8)
Total	26,782 (100)	28,366 (100)	32,909 (100)	38,218 (100)	45,986 (100)	61,179 (100)

Source: Census and Statistics Department.
Note: Column percentages in brackets.

Table 3.5 illustrates the lack of consistency that characterizes the application of eligibility criteria. It shows the waiting periods of applicants for one-way permits who were admitted into Hong Kong in 1995 and 1996. While nearly half of the applicants waited for less than two years before entering Hong Kong, a considerable number waited for ten years, and even over twenty years.

Because of the huge backlog of eligible applicants for one-way permits and the long waiting period for approval, there has been enormous pressure to allocate quotas in favour of family reunion. However, Table 3.6 shows that a sizeable proportion of those who were issued one-way permits in fact had no next-of-kin in Hong Kong and therefore were not approved for the purpose of family reunion. The number of these immigrants of unknown eligibility in 1991 was as high as 2,530 (9.4% of all immigrants). This percentage gradually fell to 3.8% in 1996 as the pressure for family reunion mounted. According to the eligibility criteria established in 1986,

Table 3.7

Agreed-upon Quotas versus Actual Arrivals, 1991–96

Year	Quota	Actual Arrival	Difference
1991	27,375	26,800	–575
1992	27,375	28,400	+1,025
1993	27,375	32,909	+5,534
1994*	38,325	38,218	–107
1995**	46,538	45,986	–552
1996	54,750	61,179	+6,429
Total	221,738	233,492	+11,754

Source: *Oriental Daily News*, 17 May 1997

Note: *Daily quota increased from 75 to 105 on 1 January 1994.
          **Daily quota increased to 150 on 1 July 1995.

applicants in categories (1) to (3) certainly will have next-of-kin in Hong Kong. Applicants in category (4) who are sole inheritors of estates of deceased relatives in Hong Kong may or may not have next-of-kin in Hong Kong. In any case, the number in this category should be small. It is logical to conclude that the sizeable group of immigrants of unknown eligibility falls under category (5) — other applicants with special considerations. It is unconscionable to allow this category to take up such a large percentage of the quota when the pressure for reunion of separated families is so strong and when the average waiting period is so long. The processing of one-way permits for applicants with special considerations under category (5) is prone to corruption.

The Chinese government apparently also has difficulty keeping to the agreed quota. Table 3.7 shows that from 1991 to 1996 the number of actual arrivals exceeded the aggregate quota by 11,754. The difference between the number of actual arrivals and the annual quota fluctuated considerably. In 1996 the excess was as high as 6,429.

Another problem with the allocation of quotas is that the Chinese authorities treat applicants individually rather than treating a family as a unit. Consequently, there have been many instances of young children being issued one-way permits to come to Hong

Kong but not their mothers. The entry of young children into Hong Kong without their mothers creates numerous single-parent families on this side of the border. This defeats the purpose of family reunion. Child care within these families in Hong Kong becomes a problem. There have been many instances of low-income fathers giving up employment to stay home to care for their children and relying on Comprehensive Social Security Assistance (CSSA) for support. Media coverage of such cases has aroused acrimony within the Hong Kong community toward increased immigration.

In summary, the processing of applications by the Chinese authorities for one-way permits within the agreed-upon quota has been poorly co-ordinated, inefficiently managed, and executed without transparency, consistency, or accountability. This has resulted in injustice and caused much anguish in the families concerned. It has given rise to plenty of opportunities for corruption to breed and for rumours to spread, which snake heads exploit to their advantage.

In response to criticism and pressure, in May 1997 the Ministry of Public Security in Beijing announced a new computerized point system for the approval of one-way permits to be adhered to by all approving authorities in China. This new system reclassifies the categories of eligible applicants. Children are taken out of the former category (3) and classified separately as "children going to Hong Kong to be under the care of their relatives there". The point system heavily favours the reunion of husbands and wives, assigning 0.1 point for every day of separation or 36.5 points for one year of separation. The approved applicant may bring one child under the age of fourteen to Hong Kong. On the other hand, the points assigned to children going to Hong Kong to be reunited with their immediate family members are 15 plus (15 minus age of child). In other words, the maximum points possible is 30. This new system still treats each applicant individually instead of treating the family as a unit.

This new system has the merit of transparency, as all applicants can calculate their scores. In Beijing, the prevailing cutting point scores for the approval of one-way permits are actually publicly

Table 3.8

Overseas Chinese Employees and Their Family Members
Admitted into Hong Kong on Employment Visas, 1993–94

	1993	1994
Employees	192	334
Family Members	119	153
Total	311	487

Source: See text.

announced. For the first time since one-way permits to Hong Kong have been issued, applicants can obtain some idea of where they stand in the queue and estimate how long they will have to wait before being assigned a one-way permit. It remains to be seen whether this new point system will be uniformly implemented among approving authorities in the various provinces and whether it will be adhered to, but it is certainly a step in the right direction.

Immigration and Employment

Besides immigrating to Hong Kong by way of the one-way permits that are allocated predominantly for family reunion, Chinese citizens may enter Hong Kong and gain residence status through employment. There are three major schemes of immigration through employment. Entry under each of these is outside the daily quota of one-way permits. The three schemes are discussed in the following three sub-sections:

Overseas Chinese Citizens Originally from the Mainland

In response to the large outflow of professional and skilled personnel from Hong Kong through emigration in the 1980s (see Chapter 5), in 1990 the Hong Kong government broadened the coverage of overseas professional and skilled personnel who can come to Hong Kong to work on employment visas to include overseas Chinese citizens. Hitherto, the Immigration Regulations have allowed foreign professional and skilled personnel but not overseas Chinese citizens who have been offered employment by employers in Hong Kong to come to Hong Kong to work on jobs approved by the Immigration Department on employment visas. Such entry is not limited by quotas. These overseas employees are granted a conditional stay in Hong Kong, which is converted to an unconditional stay after continuous residence of seven years. Under the terms of an unconditional stay, overseas employees can re-enter Hong Kong without entry visas as long as their period of absence from Hong Kong does not exceed one year.

In September 1990, with the agreement of the Chinese authorities, the Hong Kong government allowed Chinese citizens who had resided overseas for two years or more to enter Hong Kong with employment visas as long as they possessed professional skills that were needed and had been offered employment by Hong Kong employers, in line with other foreign employees. These overseas Chinese employees are granted a conditional stay in Hong Kong; they are restricted from being employed as civil servants; they are not allowed to study in Hong Kong; and they are not allowed to change jobs without the approval of the Immigration Department. After seven years of continuous residence, they can apply to become permanent residents of Hong Kong like those admitted with one-way permits. Table 3.8 shows the number of overseas Chinese employees and their family members admitted in 1993 and 1994.

Employees of Enterprises of Chinese Capital from the Mainland

Enterprises in Hong Kong that are established with Chinese capital from the Mainland are allowed to recruit employees from the Mainland and bring them to Hong Kong to work on employment visas. The criteria for the issuance of employment visas used by the Immigration Department are the same as those for other foreign and overseas Chinese employees. There is neither an overall quota restriction nor a restriction on the number for each enterprise. After seven years of continuous residence, these employees from the Mainland can apply to become permanent residents of Hong Kong.

On 27 May 1996 the Assistant Director of Immigration revealed in a Legislative Council meeting that there were about 10,000 such employees in Hong Kong.

Professional and Skilled Personnel from the Mainland

In 1994 the Executive Council approved the implementation of a pilot importation scheme of Mainland professional and skilled personnel with an annual quota of 1,000. The pilot scheme was to be reviewed after one year. If the total number of applications exceeds 1,000, the quota will be assigned in four quarterly batches of 250 by lottery. Employers may identify suitable candidates through one of the three designated labour service agencies in China. Contracts are for a duration of two years and must be approved by the Ministry of Foreign Economic Relation and Trade and the Hong Kong and Macau Office in the State Council. When the contracts are approved, the agents can apply for passports from the Ministry of Public Security and for employment visas from the British Embassy in China.

Candidates for importation are restricted to graduates of the 36 key universities designated by the Commission of Education in the Mainland. These candidates are assessed with respect to whether they have the skills and experience relevant to the jobs for which they are employed. They are not allowed to bring their families to Hong Kong, but they can break the initial contract and change jobs. After seven years of continuous residence, they can apply to become permanent residents of Hong Kong.

The progress of the implementation of this importation scheme has been slow. The business sector's initial response to the scheme was enthusiastic, with 3,129 applications bidding for the quota of 1,000. However, 1,400 applications were subsequently withdrawn. By February 1997, almost three years after the scheme was launched, the quota of 1,000 had not been used up. Only 689 applications were approved, and among them 597 arrived in Hong Kong for employment (*Ming Pao*, 5 January 1998). They are distributed mainly in the export–import, construction, and manufacturing and finance industries. The imported personnel have taken up employment primarily as managers, engineers, administrators, and sales personnel.

Difficulty in identifying suitable candidates in the 36 designated universities; the high cost of recruitment (HK$30,000 for charges and agent fees); and the job mobility of the appointee (which reduces the incentive of the employers to invest in the costly and laborious recruitment process) are blamed for the slow progress of the scheme and the high withdrawal rate.

To summarize, in recent years the Hong Kong government has opened up another channel besides family reunion by which Chinese citizens can immigrate into Hong Kong. That new channel is employment. This has redressed to some extent the previous imbalance between virtually unlimited admission of foreign professional and skilled personnel from countries other than China for employment in Hong Kong, and the prohibition of Chinese personnel from the Mainland from entering Hong Kong for the same purpose. However, the entry of Chinese professional and skilled personnel from the Mainland is confined within the remit of the last two schemes described above. The Hong Kong government's main concern has been that an unrestricted scheme similar to the one in practice for other foreign employees would bring in an uncontrollable inflow of Chinese employees, many of whom may be relatives or friends of their sponsors in Hong Kong rather than actual employees. This would open the floodgate for Chinese citizens to circumvent the quota restriction to immigrate to Hong Kong. It is also very hard to police overstaying in Hong Kong of employees from the Mainland after their contracts expire. For these same reasons, the Hong Kong government has so far disallowed the importation of domestic helpers from the Mainland. In comparison, importation from the Philippines has been unlimited, resulting in some 130,000 Filipino domestic helpers working in Hong Kong in 1997.

CHAPTER 4

Characteristics of Chinese Immigrants

Society of Immigrants

We define immigrants to be individuals who were not born in Hong Kong and who at some point in time came to Hong Kong to take up residence. In contrast, natives are individuals who were born in Hong Kong. The 1981 Census shows that at that time 37% of the Hong Kong population were immigrants from the Mainland. This percentage fell somewhat to 35.6 in 1991 and to 32.6 in 1996 as a result of the restriction after 1980 that limited the daily intake of legal immigrants (see Table 4.1). Together with another 7.1% of the population born in places other than the Mainland, the foreign-born made up almost 40% of the Hong Kong population in 1996.

In 1996 the 7.1% of the population who were born outside Hong Kong and the Mainland were mostly expatriate employees and their dependents, foreign workers, and domestic helpers. Their stay in Hong Kong is transient. In contrast, among the 32.6% of the population who were born in the Mainland, many have been in Hong Kong for more than seven years and are for permanent resident status. They originally entered Hong Kong by way of a variety of channels, including illegal ones prior to the abolition of the reached-base policy in 1980. Most came with work visas, two-way entry permits, or one-way entry permits. Regardless of the means of entry into Hong Kong, they have obtained resident or permanent resident status. They are in the proper sense immigrants, in contrast to the aforementioned 7.1% of the population born

Table 4.1
Hong Kong Population by Place of Birth

Place of Birth	1981 Number	1981 %	1991 Number	1991 %	1996 Number	1996 %
Hong Kong	3,203,200	59.4	3,299,600	59.8	3,749,300	60.3
China	1,999,200	37.0	1,967,500	35.6	2,026,200	32.6
Others	193,600	3.6	255,200	4.6	442,100	7.1
Total	5,396,000	100.0	5,522,300	100.0	6,217,600	100.0

Source: Hong Kong Census and By-Census, 1981, 1991, 1996.

outside Hong Kong and the Mainland. In this book we will focus on Chinese immigrants only.

Conceptually, it is useful to categorize Chinese immigrants into earlier and recent Chinese immigrants. Census datasets contain information on place of birth, thus identifying individuals as native-born or as immigrants from the Mainland. The 1991 Census and the 1996 By-Census queried the year of immigration. However, the 1981 Census reported only the address of respondents five years before the census was taken. So for 1981 we can determine only whether immigrants entered Hong Kong less than six years before the census was taken, or earlier. Due to this practical constraint on information available in the census, it is convenient to classify "recent" Chinese immigrants as those who were born in the Mainland and who had resided in Hong Kong for less than six years at the time of the census, and "earlier" Chinese immigrants as those who were born in the Mainland and had resided in Hong Kong for six years or longer at the time of the census. It should be noted that some earlier Chinese immigrants may have resided in Hong Kong for several decades, but at one point early in their lives they left the Mainland and entered Hong Kong as immigrants. They should therefore be classified as immigrants even though they might have fully integrated into Hong Kong society after several decades of residence.

There are two reasons why earlier and recent immigrants may be different from one another. First, they may be different in terms of socioeconomic characteristics. The former may be integrated into the Hong Kong society and may exhibit characteristics akin to the native-born, whereas the latter, being relatively new in the territory, are more like Mainland residents. Second, besides changing as a result of assimilation, earlier immigrants may be different from recent immigrants because of a cohort effect. The cohort of recent immigrants who arrived in Hong Kong in 1996 may be different from the cohort of recent immigrants who arrived earlier due to the change in immigration policy and the selection mechanism over time. By 1996 the cohorts of recent immigrants who arrived in Hong Kong in 1991 or earlier would have become earlier immigrants by definition. Hence, if the immigrant cohorts of different arrival years are different in terms of their characteristics, earlier and recent immigrants in any particular census year would, *ceteris paribus*, be different.

From 1981 to 1996, owing to the abolition of the reached-base policy, the share of recent Chinese immigrants in the population halved, falling from 6% in 1981 to 2.8% in 1991 and to 3.2% in 1996. The share of the natives increased, and that of earlier Chinese immigrants declined slightly. The group of "others" gained substantially; its share in the population doubled from 3.6% in 1981 to 7.1% in 1996, reflecting a substantial internationalization of Hong Kong's labour force and population.

Social Characteristics of Chinese Immigrants

Table 4.2 compares characteristics of natives, earlier Chinese immigrants, and recent Chinese immigrants. The table is based on a 20% sample micro-data of the 1981 Census, a 5% sample of the 1991 Census, and the 100% full sample of 1996 By-Census. Analyses in the subsequent chapters of this book are based on these datasets.

Gender

Across the three censuses the gender ratio of natives is quite balanced, with a male-to-female ratio of about fifty-one to forty-nine.

Chapter 4

Table 4.2
Social Characteristics of Chinese Immigrants
(%)

Characteristics	Hong Kong Natives			Earlier Immigrants			Recent Immigrants		
	1981	1991	1996	1981	1991	1996	1981	1991	1996
Gender									
Male	50.6	51.0	51.8	52.1	52.9	52.5	58.4	39.1	41.9
Female	49.4	49.0	48.2	47.9	47.1	47.5	41.6	60.9	58.1
Age									
0– 4	13.3	9.8	8.1	0.0	0.0	0.0	4.1	4.6	7.8
5–14	26.6	22.2	18.4	2.1	1.9	2.1	16.6	21.3	19.3
15–24	32.3	20.7	18.3	5.4	5.8	6.2	36.3	18.5	14.3
25–34	17.5	25.4	22.4	16.0	11.5	9.4	21.7	23.5	26.1
35–44	4.0	14.0	19.3	17.6	18.4	17.4	11.2	17.0	17.2
45–54	3.2	3.3	6.9	23.3	18.2	19.0	5.4	7.3	7.5
55–64	1.8	2.7	3.4	19.2	21.6	19.0	2.6	4.6	4.4
Over 64	1.3	1.9	3.2	16.4	22.6	27.0	2.1	3.2	3.4
Average age (years)	19.2	23.8	27.4	47.9	50.1	51.7	25.3	27.7	27.9
Married Status									
Married	22.5	32.6	37.6	72.4	73.0	71.3	35.4	49.8	51.8
Not married	77.5	67.4	62.4	27.6	27.0	28.7	64.6	50.2	48.2
Usual Language									
Cantonese	n.a.	98.4	98.8	n.a.	84.0	85.2	n.a.	52.8	56.7
Other Chinese dialects	n.a.	1.6	1.2	n.a.	16.0	14.8	n.a.	47.2	43.3
Educational Attainment									
No Schooling	12.4	9.0	7.3	27.5	24.3	19.9	10.0	8.8	6.8
Kindergarten	7.5	6.6	5.5	0.1	0.0	0.0	3.7	5.8	8.6
Primary	33.0	26.2	23.3	43.4	36.4	35.0	39.9	33.0	29.2
F.1–F.3	20.1	19.3	19.7	12.3	18.0	19.5	25.5	25.2	24.4
F.4–F.5	19.0	24.9	25.7	11.0	13.8	14.7	14.8	15.6	14.2
F.6–F.7	3.4	4.3	4.9	1.4	2.3	3.5	1.6	3.1	4.8
Non-degree course	3.0	5.7	5.4	2.0	2.3	2.5	1.5	3.0	3.0
First degree course	1.4	3.7	7.0	2.1	2.8	4.4	2.8	5.3	7.4
Postgraduate course	0.2	0.3	1.2	0.2	0.2	0.5	0.2	0.3	1.6
Average schooling (years)	6.5	7.6	8.3	5.3	6.0	6.5	6.6	7.2	7.4
Housing									
Public rental housing	n.a.	44.0	39.8	n.a.	41.6	43.4	n.a.	11.9	21.6
Public housing (sale)	n.a.	8.9	13.6	n.a.	5.9	9.6	n.a.	2.3	3.4
Self-contained private housing	n.a.	36.3	36.4	n.a.	41.6	38.8	n.a.	66.4	61.5
Non-self-contained private housing	n.a.	8.0	8.8	n.a.	5.3	5.0	n.a.	6.7	5.3
Others	n.a.	2.8	1.4	n.a.	5.6	3.2	n.a.	12.7	8.2

Source: Hong Kong Census 1981, 1991, By-census 1996. Sample datasets.
Note: Except for "average age" and "average schooling", all figures are column percentages.

Among earlier Chinese immigrants the gender ratio is also rather stable over time, with a ratio of about fifty-two to forty-eight throughout in favour of the male. Most of the earlier immigrants were illegal immigrants who arrived in Hong Kong at least six years before the census date. The cohorts are male dominated because of self-selection. Specifically, the massive influx of illegal immigrants who crossed the border into Hong Kong between 1978 and 1980 before the abolition of the reached-base policy were predominantly male. They were considered to be recent immigrants in the 1981 Census but became earlier immigrants in the 1991 Census. This sudden abrupt surge of the male population accounts for the 0.8% increase in the male ratio of earlier immigrants in 1991 over 1981.

The impact of the influx of illegal immigrants from 1978 to 1980 on the gender composition is most apparent among recent immigrants. In 1981 the male-to-female ratio of fifty-eight to forty-two was highly skewed in favour of the male, mainly because of the influx of illegal immigrants who were predominantly male before the reached-base policy was abolished in October 1980. In 1991 the gender ratio completely reversed to a male-to female ratio of thirty-nine to sixty-one. This is mainly attributable to a shift in the immigration policy from one that allowed illegal immigrants to take up residence prior to October 1980 to one that restricted entry and residence to legal immigrants only. The high ratio of females in the 1991 Census and the 1996 By-Census indicates that legal immigrants are being admitted into Hong Kong mainly for the purpose of family reunion. Many of the legal immigrants admitted in recent years are wives of Hong Kong residents who immigrated to Hong Kong to join their husbands.

The predominance of females among recent immigrants who entered Hong Kong for family reunion in recent years will have important implications for the future labour supply in Hong Kong.

Age

Over the 1980s the native population of Hong Kong aged considerably. There has been a clear shift in the age structure of the native population towards older age groups. The fall in the percentage of children and teenagers in the native population from 1981 to 1996 was drastic (see Table 4.2). As we will explain in Chapter 5, the ageing of the native population is mainly the result of a rather rapid decline in fertility and of a moderate decline in the death rate.

Relative to natives, there are very few children and teenagers among the earlier immigrants in the 1981, 1991, and 1996 cohorts. By virtue of self selection, the illegal Chinese immigrants who arrived prior to the abolition of the reached-base policy were mostly young men and not children or teenagers. After immigration was restricted to those who had legal status, children and teenagers were not admitted in any significant numbers until the mid-1980s. Hence it is not expected that their share among the stock of earlier immigrants will increase to any significant extent in future.

The age pattern of recent immigrants is quite different from the natives' age pattern. So have been the changes of that pattern for the two groups from 1981 to 1996. Among both natives and recent immigrants, there has been a slight increase in the percentage of the 65-plus age group. However, unlike the native group's situation, the proportion of children and teenagers among recent immigrants has increased substantially, reflecting a shift in the selection criteria of the Chinese authorities in favour of family reunion.

The percentage of recent immigrants of working age (15–64) fell from 77.2% in 1981 to 69.5% in 1996. Over the same period, the percentage of this group within the native population increased substantially, from 58.8% to 70.3%. The increase in the proportion of children, teenagers, and retirees among recent immigrants in the recent arrival cohorts will have implications for Hong Kong's labour supply in both the short run and the long run.

Marital Status

The percentage of married individuals among natives and earlier immigrants increased from 1981 to 1996. This is the natural consequence of the ageing of the population. The percentage of married individuals among recent immigrants increased drastically too, from 35.4% in the 1981 cohort to 51.8% in the 1996 cohort. The magnitude of the increase far exceeds that of the increase in the percentage of married people among natives, despite the fact that the 1991 cohort has a larger percentage of children and teenagers (see Table 4.2). This is again reflective of the admission of a higher proportion of married women when immigration priorities shifted toward family reunion.

Language

Whilst the native population is predominantly Cantonese speaking (98.4%), Cantonese-speaking recent immigrants represent only slightly over half (56.7%) of the 1996 cohort (see Table 4.2). Over 40% of the recent immigrants speak Putonghua (Mandarin) or other Chinese dialects. This will have implications for their assimilation into the Hong Kong community in general and into the labour market in particular.

The percentage of earlier immigrants in the 1996 cohort who speak Cantonese is very high (85.2%), though not as high as the corresponding percentage of natives. It is not clear that this high percentage is largely a result of the self-selection of illegal immigrants who originated mainly in Guangdong, or of their learning of Cantonese after residing in Hong Kong.

Schooling

Across the three censuses, there has been an improvement in educational opportunities in Hong Kong. Table 4.2 shows a significant reduction in the percentage of natives with primary schooling or lower and a marked increase in the percentage of those with secondary schooling and first-degree courses.

It is significant that earlier immigrants have in general a much lower level of educational attainment than natives and recent immigrants. Specifically, according to the three censuses, as many as 20% to 28% of earlier immigrants have had no schooling, and 35% to 43% with only primary education. The high percentages (55% to 71%) of earlier immigrants with poor education are indicative of the low educational attainment of the adult illegal immigrants, who mostly made up the earlier immigrant cohorts. In other words, besides being predominantly young males by virtue of self-selection, most illegal immigrants had very little education, which affected their employment opportunities and their earnings in the Hong Kong labour market. There was a slight improvement in the educational attainment profile of the earlier immigrant cohort from 1981 to 1996. This is partly due to the acquisition of further schooling after immigration into Hong Kong and partly due to the admission of legal immigrants after October 1980. These immigrants are identified as earlier immigrants in the 1991 Census and the 1996 By-Census. As we will show, legal immigrants admitted into Hong Kong after 1980 generally had a higher level of educational attainment than those who entered Hong Kong earlier.

A comparison of the 1981 cohort of recent immigrants and the 1981 cohort of earlier immigrants shows that the former has a higher educational attainment level, despite the fact that it contains a much higher percentage (20.7%) of children (aged fourteen and under) than the former (2.1%). The 1981 cohort of recent immigrants is made up of mostly (but not exclusively) illegal immigrants who entered Hong Kong after 1975. This more recent cohort of illegal immigrants apparently has a much higher level of educational attainment than previous cohorts of illegal immigrants who entered Hong Kong before 1975 and who are classified as earlier immigrants in the 1981 census.

The educational attainment level of recent immigrants shows further improvement from the 1981 cohort to the 1996 cohort. In contrast to the former cohort, the latter is made up of exclusively legal immigrants. It is clear that legal immigrants are better educated than illegal ones. The mechanism through which they are selected is different from the self-selection mechanism applied to illegal immigrants. Illegal immigrants are less educated than the legal ones, probably because the opportunity cost of being caught after illegal entry and repatriated to China has been lower for those with little education than for those better educated ones with careers in the Mainland. Despite the fact that the proportion of children aged under 15 in the 1996 cohort of recent immigrants is significantly higher than that in the 1981 cohort, the percentage of individuals with primary schooling or less in the 1996 cohort is only 44.6%, as compared to 53.6% in 1981. Correspondingly, the proportion of individuals with senior secondary schooling, first degrees, and postgraduate degrees in 1996 is higher than that in 1981.

It should be noted that the 1996 cohort of recent immigrants includes all immigrants who arrived in Hong Kong after 1990. Some of the immigrants, especially the younger ones, would have acquired more schooling in Hong Kong after arrival. The statistics shown in Table 4.2 include both schooling acquired in the Mainland before arrival and schooling acquired in Hong Kong after arrival. A better portrayal of the educational background of new immigrants upon arrival in Hong Kong is given in Table 4.3, which shows the educational attainment of immigrants by year of arrival in Hong Kong from 1991 to 1996. The increase in the percentage of new immigrants with no schooling, with kindergarten, or with primary schooling from 1991 to 1996 reflects the shift in the composition of immigrants admitted in recent years towards a higher percentage of children. Overall, the educational attainment of new immigrants from 1991 to 1996, as shown in Table 4.3, is lower than that of the 1996 cohort of recent immigrants reported in Table 4.2. The improvement in the educational attainment profile reflected in Table 4.2 over that reflected in Table 4.3 indicates that new immigrants, especially younger ones, acquired more schooling in Hong Kong after their arrival. For instance, Table 4.2 shows that 12% of the cohort of recent immigrants in 1996 (arriving between 1991 and 1996) have had post-secondary education, whereas Table 4.3 indicates only 5.4% to 10.8% of the new immigrants *on arrival* (from 1991 to 1996) had that. The difference is accounted for by acquisition of schooling in Hong Kong after arrival.

To summarize, even before the curtailment of the inflow of illegal immigrants after 1980, more recent cohorts of illegal recent immigrants appear to be better educated than the earlier cohorts. This may reflect improved educational opportunities in the

Table 4.3

Educational Attainment of Legal Immigrants from China who Entered Hong Kong by Year of Arrival, 1991–96

Educational Attainment	Year of Arrival					
	1991	1992	1993	1994	1995	1996
University / post-secondary	2,689 (10.0)	3,065 (10.8)	3,541 (10.8)	3,527 (9.2)	3,232 (7.0)	3,293 (5.4)
Secondary	10,996 (41.1)	11,859 (41.8)	14,008 (42.6)	17,080 (44.7)	19 357 (42.6)	22,404 (36.6)
Primary	7,891 (29.5)	8,055 (28.4)	10,073 (30.6)	11,254 (29.4)	13,634 (29.6)	20,953 (34.2)
No schooling / kindergarten	5,116 (19.1)	5,354 (18.9)	5,251 (16.0)	6,315 (16.5)	9,542 (20.7)	14,529 (23.7)
Unknown	90 (0.3)	33 (0.1)	36 (0.1)	42 (0.1)	0 (0.0)	0 (0.0)
Total	26,782 (100.0)	28,366 (100.0)	32,909 (100.0)	38,218 (100.0)	45,986 (100.0)	61,179 (100.0)

Source: Census and Statistics Department, Hong Kong.
Note: Column percentage in parentheses.

Mainland, where they obtained their schooling over time. In particular, recent immigrants who entered Hong Kong legally after 1980 are better educated than those who entered illegally before 1980. As we will show in Chapter 7, the more recent cohorts of immigrants who are better educated is better assimilated into the labour market of Hong Kong than the earlier cohorts.

Housing

As a result of the Hong Kong government's public housing policy, in 1996 as many as 39.8% of Hong Kong natives lived in public rental housing. The percentage of earlier immigrants in public rental housing is slightly higher, at 43.4%, probably because their income in general is lower than the natives'. Recent immigrants who, by definition, have been in Hong Kong for less than six years, do not meet the eligibility criterion of seven years of residence in Hong Kong for allocation of public rental housing units. Consequently, only 11.9% of recent immigrants reported residence in public rental housing in 1991, but the figure increased to 21.6% in 1996. Those who reported living in public rental housing were probably staying with relatives who lived in public rental units. The increase in the percentage from 1991 to 1996 perhaps reflects the shift toward family reunion in the selection criteria. Mainland wives and their children reunite with their husbands and fathers, who most probably reside in public rental housing.

Economic Characteristics of Chinese Immigrants

Economic Activity Status

The labour force participation rate of male and female natives (aged 15–64) increased from 1981 to 1996 (see Table 4.4). In contrast, the corresponding labour force participation rates for male earlier immigrants fell slightly because a higher proportion of them were full-time students or retirees in 1996 as compared with the proportion in 1981 (see Table 4.5). It is interesting to note that despite the decline in labour force participation rates over time, the participation rate of male earlier immigrants is still slightly higher than that of male natives. This is consistent with the interpretation that immigrants are highly motivated to seek employment in the destination country to earn a living to support themselves and their families. The labour force participation rate of female earlier immigrants is, however, rising, but it is substantially lower than that of female natives. The lower rate is presumably due to their greater difficulty in securing employment in Hong Kong's labour market. Consequently, a much larger proportion of them become homemakers than female natives.

The labour force participation rates of both male and female recent immigrants of working age (15–64) in 1981 are substantially higher than those of the natives. The rate for male recent immigrants in 1981 was as high as 95.8% (see Table 4.4). This reflects the self-selected nature of the 1981 cohort. At that time, recent immigrants were mostly illegal. They had left their homeland and risked their lives to cross the border to look for better economic

Table 4.4
Labour Force Participation Rate (15–64 Age Group)

	Natives (%)			Earlier Immigrants (%)			Recent Immigrants (%)		
	1981	1991	1996	1981	1991	1996	1981	1991	1996
Labour force participation									
All	66.5	72.8	70.4	63.8	66.3	65.2	85.3	66.3	61.0
Male	77.4	84.2	84.8	85.6	85.7	83.2	95.8	82.7	82.3
Female	55.7	61.1	61.1	40.2	41.9	43.1	69.9	58.0	48.4
Economically inactive									
All	33.5	27.2	27.2	36.2	33.7	34.8	14.7	33.6	39.0
Male	22.6	15.8	15.8	14.4	14.3	16.8	4.2	17.3	17.7
Female	44.3	38.9	40.6	59.8	58.1	56.9	30.1	42.0	51.6

Source:See Table 4.2.

opportunities in Hong Kong. Hence, almost all of them were economically active after arrival in Hong Kong.

However, the rates for both male and female recent immigrants declined substantially from 1981 to 1996, with a drop of 13.5 percentage points and 21.5 percentage points for males and females, respectively. The decline for female recent immigrants was so extreme that by 1991 their labour force participation rates had fallen below those of natives. This substantial decline is a result of the drastic change in the composition of recent immigrants. Unlike the 1981 cohort, the 1996 cohort of recent immigrants is exclusively composed of legal immigrants, with a larger percentage of children and married women who entered Hong Kong to be reunited with their family. Table 4.5 shows that the percentage of students and homemakers who are economically inactive (they do not participate in the labour force) increased substantially from the 1981 cohort of recent immigrants to the 1996 cohort. Specifically, 24.8% of female recent immigrants in 1981 were homemakers. By 1996 this percentage of homemakers had increased to 40.2%.

It is interesting to analyze further the difference in the distribution of natives and immigrants in terms of whether they are

Table 4.5
Economic Activity Status of the 15–64 Age Group
(%)

Natives Activity Status	1981			1991			1996		
	All	Male	Female	All	Male	Female	All	Male	Female
Employee	56.3	65.2	47.4	63.6	71.9	55.1	60.2	66.6	53.1
Self-employed	2.0	3.0	1.0	2.6	3.9	1.3	2.5	3.5	1.3
Hawker	0.7	0.9	0.5	n.a.	n.a.	n.a.	0.3	0.4	0.2
Others	1.3	2.1	0.5	n.a.	n.a.	n.a.	2.2	3.2	1.1
Employer	1.4	2.4	0.4	3.2	5.1	1.2	3.9	6.0	1.6
Unemployed	2.0	2.4	1.6	2.6	2.9	2.4	3.2	3.9	2.5
Homemaker / housewife	12.4	0.3	24.5	11.8	0.2	23.8	11.5	0.2	23.8
Full-time student	17.2	18.0	16.4	12.5	12.6	12.4	11.9	11.4	12.5
Retired	1.5	2.1	1.0	1.3	1.4	1.3	1.7	1.6	1.8
Others	7.2	8.7	7.7	2.4	2.0	1.7	5.1	6.8	3.4
Total	100.0	100.0	100.0	100.0	100.0	100.0	100.0	100.0	100.0

Earlier Immigrants Activity Status	1981			1991			1996		
	All	Male	Female	All	Male	Female	All	Male	Female
Employee	46.9	63.3	29.1	53.4	67.7	35.3	51.9	64.1	36.8
Self-employed	6.4	9.7	2.8	5.1	7.5	2.1	3.8	5.5	1.5
Hawker	3.0	4.0	1.8	n.a.	n.a.	n.a.	0.8	1.0	0.4
Others	3.4	5.7	1.0	n.a.	n.a.	n.a.	3.0	4.5	1.1
Employer	3.6	6.4	0.6	4.9	7.6	1.4	5.7	8.8	1.9
Unemployed	1.7	2.3	1.0	2.1	2.5	1.4	3.2	4.5	1.6
Homemaker / housewife	24.3	0.7	49.9	19.1	0.6	42.3	18.2	0.4	40.1
Full-time student	0.9	0.9	0.8	3.4	3.2	3.6	3.6	3.4	3.9
Retired	9.4	11.6	7.0	8.4	7.8	9.1	9.3	8.4	10.3
Others	6.8	5.1	8.8	3.6	3.1	4.8	4.3	4.9	3.9
Total	100.0	100.0	100.0	100.0	100.0	100.0	100.0	100.0	100.0

Recent Immigrants Activity Status	1981			1991			1996		
	All	Male	Female	All	Male	Female	All	Male	Female
Employee	76.5	86.4	61.9	59.0	71.8	52.4	53.6	71.1	43.3
Self-employed	1.8	2.5	0.7	1.7	3.0	1.0	1.0	1.5	0.6
Hawker	1.0	1.4	0.3	n.a.	n.a.	n.a.	0.1	0.1	0.1
Others	0.8	1.1	0.4	n.a.	n.a.	n.a.	0.9	1.4	0.5
Employer	0.5	0.7	0.2	2.0	4.3	0.8	2.6	4.9	1.3
Unemployed	2.0	2.3	1.5	2.8	3.3	2.6	3.3	4.5	2.6
Homemaker / housewife	10.2	0.3	24.8	20.8	0.2	31.5	25.4	0.3	40.2
Full-time student	1.8	1.7	1.9	9.2	14.4	6.5	8.2	11.6	6.3
Retired	1.2	0.9	1.7	1.7	1.1	2.0	1.9	1.4	2.1
Others	6.0	5.2	7.3	2.8	1.9	2.0	4.0	4.7	3.6
Total	100.0	100.0	100.0	100.0	100.0	100.0	100.0	100.0	100.0

Source:　See Table 4.2.

employees, self-employed, employers, or unemployed. This will be done in Chapter 7 in connection with the analysis of the economic performance of immigrants in the labour market.

Employment by Occupation

The economic restructuring of the Hong Kong economy in the 1980s had an important impact on the occupational distribution of the labour force. As the manufacturing industry relocates its production facilities across the border into South China, manufacturing employment has been shrinking steadily. From 1981 to 1996 employment in Hong Kong's manufacturing industry fell from 905,000 to 325,000. During the same period, employment in the service sector, which encompasses export, import, wholesale, retail, transport, storage, communication, hotel, finance, business services, and social and personal services, increased dramatically from 835,000 to 1,954,000. Production jobs in the manufacturing industry are being eliminated and replaced by service jobs.

The shift in the occupational distribution of natives from 1981 to 1996 vividly reflects the structural transformation of the economy. The proportion of production workers fell by 28 percentage points — from 48.2% to 20.8% across the three censuses. This drop is matched by an increase in professional and administrative workers (10% to 33.7%), and by slight increases in the percentage of clerical and sales workers (see Table 4.6).

It is interesting to note that earlier immigrants are less adaptive to structural changes in the labour market than Hong Kong natives. In 1996 a larger fraction of earlier immigrants than that of the native population were still tied to the declining manufacturing industry as production workers. That fraction was 0.51 for the earlier immigrants in 1996 but only 0.21 for the natives that year. The gain in the proportion of earlier immigrants working in a professional or administrative capacity has also been less significant than the corresponding gain for the natives. In general, earlier immigrants have been adjusting to the restructured labour market, but not as successfully as the natives have. This is partly because as a group they are older and therefore less adaptable to the changing demand for skills in the labour market.

In 1981 recent immigrants were predominantly employed (74.4%) as production and production-related workers, mainly in the manufacturing industry. At that time, recent immigrants were mostly illegal, young, and relatively uneducated. They were not very successful in obtaining service jobs. Unlike production jobs in manufacturing, which require mostly general skills, service sector jobs require more country-specific skills. They usually involve more intensive personal interaction, and therefore require language skills and social and cultural skills specific to a country.[1]

Skills that illegal recent Chinese immigrants in the 1981 cohort possessed were more likely to be related to agriculture or manufacturing in the Mainland than to service industries, since the service sector in the Mainland was small. While production skills in manufacturing may be general and therefore transferable from the Mainland to Hong Kong after immigration, service sector skills are more country-specific, and even if recent immigrants had such skills in the Mainland, these skills are less transferable to Hong Kong. In short, recent immigrants in 1981 were disadvantaged in terms of finding service jobs.

The trend shifted substantially for the 1991 and 1996 cohorts. The recent immigrants in these cohorts were legal, and they were better educated than the previous cohorts of recent immigrants, who mostly entered Hong Kong by illegal means. Unlike the 1981 cohort of recent immigrants who were brought up in the Mainland isolated from the outside world, the 1991 and 1996 cohorts left the Mainland after 1985 and 1990. It was a period about six to eleven years after China launched the open-door policy and economic reform. Since the opening up of China, there has been a massive flow of information between Hong Kong and the Mainland as a result of the flow of investments, visitors, and mass media across the border. The 1991 and 1996 cohorts of recent immigrants must have gained more information on the Hong Kong community in general, and the labour market in particular, than the previous cohorts did before they immigrated to Hong Kong. Their better understanding

Chapter 4

Table 4.6
Occupational Distribution of Hong Kong Population, 1981, 1991, 1996
(%)

Occupation	Natives			Earlier Immigrants			Recent Immigrants		
	1981	1991	1996	1981	1991	1996	1981	1991	1996
Professional and administrative worker	10.0	27.4	33.7	6.7	15.8	21.0	2.5	12.9	21.4
Clerical and related worker	20.1	22.7	21.9	6.5	7.7	10.4	3.0	11.3	12.3
Sales and service worker	20.1	22.2	23.0	33.4	32.1	33.9	18.8	28.8	35.4
Agriculture and fishery worker	0.1	0.4	0.6	2.2	0.7	0.5	0.8	0.2	0.4
Production and related worker	48.2	27.2	20.8	50.7	43.6	34.2	74.4	46.8	30.5
Others	1.5	0.1	0.0	0.5	0.1	0.0	0.5	0.0	0.0
Total	100.0	100.0	100.0	100.0	100.0	100.0	100.0	100.0	100.0

Source: See Table 4.2.

of the language, culture, and ethos of Hong Kong would have probably helped them in taking up jobs in the service sector. The gain in the percentage of service jobs by category of the 1991 and 1996 cohorts of recent immigrants as compared to the 1981 cohort is remarkable. The proportion of professional and administrative workers increased from 2.5% to 12.9% and 21.4%, respectively; the proportion of clerical and related workers from 3.0% to 11.3% and 12.3%, respectively; and the proportion of sales and service workers from 18.8% to 28.8% and 35.4%, respectively. However, in the interim, the proportion of production and related workers fell drastically, from 74.4% to 46.8% and 30.5% (see Table 4.6). The gain in the proportion of service sector employment of recent immigrants from 1981 to 1996 is much more significant than the gain for earlier immigrants, so much so that by 1996 the pattern of occupational distribution of recent immigrants was more service-sector oriented than the pattern for earlier immigrants. This pattern shift is significant because, fifteen years earlier, recent immigrants were much more concentrated in production jobs than earlier immigrants were at that time. In Chapter 7 we will analyse in greater depth the economic assimilation of immigrants in the labour market of Hong Kong and the importance of the cohort effect.

Table 4.6 shows the occupational distribution of recent immigrants after their arrival to Hong Kong. It is informative to compare this with the distribution of their occupations in the Mainland just prior to arrival in Hong Kong. Table 4.7 shows that the distribution of new immigrants has been heavily dominated by students and those who did not work. This was increasingly the case from 1991 to 1996. This again reflects the shift in selection criteria in favour of family reunion in recent years.

To make comparing the data presented in Table 4.6 and Table 4.7 easier, we consider only those new immigrants who worked in the Mainland before arrival in Hong Kong.

Among formerly working new immigrants, the percentage of professional, administrative, and executive workers declined slightly, from 14.4% for the 1991 arrival cohort to 13.5% for the 1996 arrival cohort. These percentages are lower than the corresponding 21.4% reported for the 1996 Census in Table 4.6. New immigrants have become more successful in moving into better occupations than they had in the Mainland. This is in line with their expectation of better economic opportunities after coming to Hong Kong.

Employment by Industry

The shift in distribution of employment by industry among natives from 1981 to 1991 by and large reflects the extent of Hong Kong's economic restructuring over the decade. Employment of natives in the manufacturing industry fell sharply, from 41.1% in 1981 to 18% in 1996. The gain in percentages in each group of service industries ranges from 3% to 8% (see Table 4.8).

Earlier immigrants were less successful in shifting out of the declining manufacturing industry. Over the period 1981 to 1996, the percentage of them employed in manufacturing fell from 39.9%

Table 4.7

**Occupation in the Mainland of Legal Immigrants from China
who Entered Hong Kong by Year of Arrival, 1991–96**

Occupation in the Mainland	Year of Arrival					
	1991	1992	1993	1994	1995	1996
Professional, administrative, and executive workers	1,638 (6.1)	2,107 (7.4)	2 058 (6.3)	2 029 (5.3)	1 829 (4.0)	1,223 (2.0)
Technicians and production workers	2,792 (10.4)	3,133 (11.0)	3,136 (9.5)	2 945 (7.7)	5 547 (12.1)	5,511 (9.0)
Farmers, hunters and fishermen	2,855 (10.7)	2,735 (9.6)	2,980 (9.1)	1,675 (4.4)	1 123 (2.4)	1,075 (1.8)
Other occupations	4,032 (15.1)	4,153 (14.6)	5,398 (16.4)	4,955 (13.0)	1,809 (3.9)	1,269 (2.1)
Students	5,686 (21.2)	5,708 (20.1)	7,055 (21.4)	8,892 (23.3)	12,196 (26.5)	18,164 (29.7)
Not working	9,773 (36.5)	10,528 (37.1)	12,280 (37.3)	17,721 (46.4)	23,482 (51.1)	33,937 (55.5)
Unknown	2 (0.02)	2 (0.007)	2 (0.006)	1 (0.003)	0 (0.0)	0 (0.0)
Total	26,782 (100.0)	28,366 (100.0)	32,909 (100.0)	38,218 (100.0)	45,986 (100.0)	61,179 (100.0)

Source:Census and Statistics Department, Hong Kong.
Note: Column percentages are put in parentheses.

to only 23.2%. In contrast, the 1996 cohort of recent immigrants, as compared with the 1981 cohort, has been rather successful at reducing its dependence on manufacturing employment. In 1981 there was a higher proportion of recent immigrants (56.7%) in manufacturing than the earlier immigrants, but by 1996 the percentage of earlier immigrants remaining in manufacturing had fallen below that of the earlier immigrants (21.6% versus 23.2%). The gain in employment in wholesale, retail, and trade was remarkable, increasing from 16% to 38.4% over the period.

Summary

To summarize, conceptually it is useful to differentiate between earlier and recent Chinese immigrants, and Hong Kong's 1981, 1991,

Table 4.8

Employment of Hong Kong Population by Industry, 1981, 1991, 1996

(%)

Industry	Natives			Earlier Immigrants			Recent Immigrants		
	1981	1991	1996	1981	1991	1996	1981	1991	1996
Agriculture, fishing, mining, quarrying	1.0	0.6	0.7	2.0	1.0	0.6	0.8	0.2	0.5
Manufacturing	41.1	25.2	18.0	39.9	33.9	23.2	56.7	46.5	21.6
Electricity, gas, water	0.8	0.9	0.8	0.5	0.5	0.6	0.3	0.1	0.2
Construction	5.7	5.0	6.7	8.6	10.6	12.9	17.3	4.5	13.7
Wholesale, retail, export, import, hotel	16.9	21.5	24.2	23.0	24.9	28.6	16.0	32.2	38.4
Transport, storage, communication	8.8	11.7	12.5	7.0	8.2	9.7	2.7	4.0	6.1
Finance, insurance, business services	7.4	13.8	15.7	2.8	6.3	9.5	0.7	4.1	8.4
Social and personal services	17.1	21.0	21.4	14.8	14.2	14.9	4.4	8.1	11.1
Others	1.2	0.3	0.0	1.4	0.4	0.0	1.1	0.3	0.0
Total	100.0	100.0	100.0	100.0	100.0	100.0	100.0	100.0	100.0

Source: See Table 4.2.

and 1996 census datasets allow us to make such a distinction. Recent immigrants who arrived in Hong Kong within six years of a census are distinctly different from the native-born in terms of their characteristics. The 1991 and 1996 cohorts of recent immigrants, who are exclusively legal, are also very different from the 1981 cohort, which is made up of mostly illegal immigrants. The newer cohorts are presumably also different from earlier cohorts of illegal immigrants. There is a higher percentage of males in the 1981 cohort than that in later ones, but there is a much lower percentage of males in the 1991 cohort as compared to that of the native population. The proportion of recent immigrants of working age (15–64) in 1981 was much higher than the corresponding proportion among natives, but by 1996 the two were about the same.

Compared with natives, recent immigrants are more likely to be married and to have less education. In 1981 a much higher proportion of recent immigrants than that of natives were economically active, but this trend reversed in 1996. Recent immigrants are likely to be production-related workers or sales and service workers. They are more likely than natives to be tied to the declining manufacturing industry in terms of employment, although an increasing proportion of recent immigrants are gaining employment in service industries such as wholesale, retail, import, export, and hotel.

The difference in the characteristics of recent immigrants and natives, and the change in characteristics of cohorts of recent immigrants over time, are important to our analysis of the contribution of Chinese immigration to Hong Kong's labour supply, the economic assimilation of immigrants, and the immigration policy. These topics will be discussed in the later chapters.

Note

1. See Chapter 7 for further development of this argument.

CHAPTER 5

Immigration, Population Growth, and Labour Supply

Natural Increase, Immigration, and Population Growth

Immigration from the Mainland has always been a major source of population growth for Hong Kong. Since World War II, each major wave of immigrants from the Mainland swelled the population. The last of these waves was the one that hit Hong Kong from 1978 to 1980. This onslaught ultimately led to the abolition of the reached-base policy in October 1980.

Since October 1980 only legal immigrants have been admitted into Hong Kong. This steady stream of legal immigrants has become an increasingly important source of population growth. Its relative importance has risen because natural increase has declined steadily and rapidly in the last three decades.

The decline in the rate of natural increase in population in Hong Kong has been a result of the rather rapid decline in fertility in Hong Kong. In 1961 the crude birth rate in Hong Kong was 35 per 1,000 persons. By 1996 it had lowered by two-thirds to 10 per 1,000 (see Table 5.1). Today, Hong Kong's total fertility rate is among the lowest in the world. Table 5.2 shows the dramatic decline from 1965 to 1990. By 1990 fertility had fallen to a low of 1.21 (children per couple), which is lower than that of virtually all North American, European, and Asian countries (see Table 5.2; Kono, 1996).

During the period 1961–96, the crude death rate dropped only slightly, from 6.1 per 1,000 persons to 4.9 per 1,000. The impact of

Chapter 5

Table 5.1
Birth Rates and Death Rates in Hong Kong, 1961–96

Year	Crude Birth Rate (per '000)	Crude Death Rate (per '000)	Rate of Natural Increase (per '000)
1961	35.0	6.1	28.9
1962	34.0	6.3	27.7
1963	33.5	5.9	27.5
1964	30.7	5.3	25.4
1965	28.1	5.0	23.1
1966	25.3	5.3	20.0
1967	23.7	5.4	18.3
1968	21.7	5.1	16.6
1969	21.3	5.0	16.4
1970	20.0	5.1	14.9
1971	19.7	5.0	14.7
1972	19.5	5.2	14.3
1973	19.4	5.0	14.4
1974	19.1	5.0	14.1
1975	17.9	4.8	13.0
1976	17.4	5.0	12.4
1977	17.5	5.1	12.4
1978	17.3	5.1	12.2
1979	16.8	5.2	11.7
1980	17.0	5.0	12.0
1981	16.8	4.8	12.0
1982	16.4	4.8	11.6
1983	15.6	5.0	10.6
1984	14.4	4.7	9.6
1985	14.0	4.6	9.3
1986	13.0	4.7	8.3
1987	12.6	4.8	7.7
1988	13.4	4.9	8.5
1989	12.3	5.1	7.2
1990	12.0	5.2	6.8
1991	12.0	5.0	7.0
1992	12.3	5.3	7.0
1993	12.0	5.2	6.8
1994	11.9	5.0	6.9
1995	11.2	5.1	6.1
1996	10.0	4.9	5.1

Note: Units are total births (or deaths) in the year, per thousand population.

Table 5.2

Total Fertility Rates of Selected Countries and Regions, 1965–90

Country	1965	1970	1975	1980	1985	1990
Asia						
Hong Kong	4.93	3.49	2.51	2.06	1.46	1.21
Japan	2.14	2.13	1.91	1.75	1.76	1.54
Singapore	4.62	3.10	2.08	1.74	1.62	1.83
South Korea	4.95	4.47	3.33	2.71	1.71	1.63
Taiwan	4.83	4.00	2.83	2.52	1.89	1.81
Northern Europe						
Denmark	2.61	1.95	1.92	1.55	1.45	1.67
Sweden	2.42	1.94	1.78	1.68	1.73	2.14
Southern Europe						
Greece	2.32	2.43	2.33	2.21	1.68	1.43*
Italy	2.55	2.46	2.19	1.66	1.41	1.29
Western Europe						
Austria	2.68	2.30	1.83	1.65	1.48	1.45
France	2.84	2.47	1.93	1.95	1.82	1.80
Germany	2.50	2.02	1.45	1.45	1.28	1.44*
Netherlands	3.04	2.58	1.66	1.60	1.51	1.62
Switzerland	2.01	2.10	1.61	1.55	1.52	1.59
United Kingdom	2.85	2.45	1.81	1.89	1.80	1.84
North America						
Canada	3.11	2.33	1.90	1.73	1.67	1.68*
United States	2.93	2.48	1.77	1.84	1.84	1.88*
Oceania						
Australia	2.98	2.86	2.22	1.92	1.89	1.90*
New Zealand	3.33	3.17	2.36	2.03	1.93	2.10*

Sources: United Nations, *Demographic Yearbook*, various years; Council of Europe, *Recent Demographic Development in the Member States of the Council of Europe*, 1990 Edition (Strasbourg, 1991); World Bank, *Social Indicators of Development 1989* (Baltimore, Maryland, The Johns Hopkins University Press, 1990); France, Institut national d'etudes demographiques; and other country population reports.

Note: Unit of total fertility rate is average number of live births per woman (couple) according to current age-specific fertility rates. *1989 figures the drastic decline in the crude birth rate on population growth was only slightly mitigated by the small decline in the crude death rate. The net effect has been a substantial decline in the rate of natural increase, from 28.9 per 1,000 persons in 1961 to less than 5.1 per 1,000 in 1996 (see Table 5.1).

As a country develops, fertility declines. This universal phenomenon has been explained by a new theory of fertility which suggests that it is a consequence of the rising value of women's time. When their labour market opportunities improve, their income increases, and the demand for child quality rises as well. All these changes make women's time more valuable than ever before. (Becker, 1981 and Willis, 1973). In this regard, there is nothing unusual about the fertility decline in Hong Kong. What is unusual is the speed of that decline. There has been little analytical research into the causes of the rapid decline in fertility in Hong Kong. However, making use of the new fertility theory as a framework of analysis, one can hypothesize that the rapid decline in fertility in Hong Kong can be explained by the rapid rise in the opportunity cost of child-rearing as well as by the rapid economic growth of Hong Kong in the last three decades. The opportunity cost is reflected in the rise in wages (female wage in particular) and housing cost. Without rigorous modelling and empirical testing of data, one cannot establish the definitive causes of the rapid decline in fertility in Hong Kong. In contrast, the mild decline in the crude death rate can be readily ascribed to better nutrition and health care in the last three decades.

The purpose of this chapter is not to ascertain the causes of the decline in the natural increase but to identify the trend of population growth. It is significant that the contribution to population growth by natural increase was only 37,000 persons in 1995. Legal immigration from the Mainland has, alone, contributed 46,000 persons that year. This was the first time since the abolition of the reached-base policy in 1980 that the contribution of immigration from China to Hong Kong's population growth exceeded the contribution of natural increase (see Table 5.3). The importance of this should not be overlooked because, given the present trend of declining fertility, legal immigration is expected to remain the *most* important source of population increase.

Emigration, Return Migration, and Volatility in Population Growth

Besides natural increase and immigration, several other factors determine the growth of population in Hong Kong. These include emigration, return migration of Hong Kong residents, and importation of expatriates and foreign workers. These other factors are either transient or volatile in nature. In Table 5.3 the net increase (decrease) in population due to factors other than natural increase is given in terms of the figures of the "balance of arrivals and departures". Arrivals include immigrants who are given residence status, return migrants, and expatriates and foreign workers, whereas departures are a result of emigration and departure of expatriates and foreign workers. These figures of the balance of arrivals and departures are rather volatile. The decade of 1960 was marked by a number of years of net outflow of population. The trend reversed in the 1970s and there was a substantial net inflow in the decade. Net arrivals of 76,000, 147,000 and 92,000, respectively, were recorded in the early years of the opening up of China: 1978, 1979, and 1980. The main cause of the bulge of net arrivals was the large influx of illegal immigrants who reached base and emerged to apply for residence in Hong Kong. After the abolition of the reached-base policy this inflow stopped.

The rising tide of emigration of Hong Kong residents following the Sino-British negotiation on the future of Hong Kong, which began in 1981, and the transitional period in the run-up to 1997 after the signing of the Sino-British Joint Declaration in 1984, kept the balance of arrivals below 30,000 throughout the 1980s. The decade ended with three years of net outflow of population of 8,000, 16,000 and 9,000, respectively, in 1988, 1989 and 1990. What is significant about the 1980s is that, had there not been a steady annual inflow of legal immigrants, there would have been a net outflow of population in each year of that decade.

Chapter 5

Table 5.3

Components of Population Growth (Excluding Vietnamese Migrants), 1961–95

Year	Estimated Population (mid-year)	Births	Deaths	Natural Increase	Balance of Arrivals & Departures*	Legal Immigrants from China
1961	3,168,100	110,884	19,325	91,559	−15,374**	n.a.
1962	3,305,200	112,503	20,933	91,570	81,260	n.a.
1963	3,420,900	114,550	20,340	94,210	−558	n.a.
1964	3,504,600	107,625	18,657	88,968	−5,737	n.a.
1965	3,597,900	101,110	18,150	82,960	−2,638	n.a.
1966	3,629,900	91,832	19,261	72,571	−18,638	n.a.
1967	3,722,800	88,215	20,234	67,981	13,271	n.a.
1968	3,802,700	82,685	19,444	63,241	20,598	n.a.
1969	3,863,900	82,482	19,256	63,226	−1,602	n.a.
1970	3,959,000	79,132	19,996	59,136	30,151	n.a.
1971	4,045,300	79,789	20,374	59,415	40,701	n.a.
1972	4,123,600	80,344	21,397	58,947	29,787	n.a.
1973	4,241,600	82,252	21,251	61,001	88,977	n.a.
1974	4,377,800	83,581	21,879	61,702	42,619	n.a.
1975	4,461,600	79,790	21,597	58,193	4,043	n.a.
1976	4,518,000	78 511	22,633	55,878	−5,711	n.a.
1977	4,583,700	80,022	23,346	56,676	23,809	n.a.
1978	4,667,500	80,957	23,830	57,127	76,117	n.a.
1979	4,870,500	81,975	25,125	56,850	147,388	n.a.
1980	5,024,400	85,290	25,008	60,282	91,708	55,452
1981	5,163,100	86,751	24,832	61,919	39,422	54,249
1982	5,253,200	86,120	25,396	60,724	23,683	53,848
1983	5,332,000	83,293	26,522	56,771	990	26,701
1984	5,385,300	77,297	25,520	51,777	2,690	27,475
1985	5,445,400	76,126	25,258	50,868	20,991	27,285
1986	5,516,300	71,620	25,912	45 708	21,059	27,111
1987	5,572,400	69,958	26,916	43,042	4,859	27,268
1988	5,609,800	75,412	27,659	47,753	−8,389	28,137
1989	5,638,500	69,621	28,745	40,876	−15,540	27,263
1990	5,649,800	67,731	29,136	38,595	−9,072	27,976
1991	5,690,800	68,281	28,429	39,852	15,613	26,782
1992	5,746,800	70,949	30,550	40,399	46,621	28,367
1993	5,860,200	70,451	30,571	39,880	83,883	32,909
1994	6,007,900	71,646	29,905	41,741	86,874	38,218
1995	6,133,000	68,637	31,468	37,169	116,322	45,986
1996	6,293,900	62,977	30,641	32,336	132,935	61,179

Source: *Hong Kong Monthly Digest of Statistics.* Demographic Statistics Section, Census and Statistics Department. Immigration Department, Hong Kong.

Note: *End-year comparison. For 1986 to 1996, the figures include an estimate of Hong Kong residents moving away to China / Macau living outside Hong Kong.
**From 7 March 1961 to 31 December 1961. n.a. means not available.

Table 5.4

Estimated Emigrants from Hong Kong by Destination Countries, 1980–96

Year	Destination Countries				
	Total	Canada	United States	Australia	Other
1980	22,400				
1981	18,300				
1982	20,300				
1983	19,800				
1984	22,400				
1985	22,300				
1986	18,989	5,615	7,742	4,441	1,191
1987	29,998	16,254	7,411	5,208	1,125
1988	45,817	24,588	11,777	7,846	1,606
1989	42,000	16,400	12,800	10,900	1,900
1990	61,700				
1991	59,700				
1992	66,200				
1993	53,400				
1994	61,600				
1995	43,100				
1996	40,300				

Source: Government Secretariat.

Note: Except for 1986 to 1989, country-breakdown data are not available.

Much of the 1980s and the early 1990s were underpinned by the rising tide of emigration. The number of emigrants was between 18,000 and 22,000 throughout the first half of the 1980s. It picked up in 1987, and rose sharply from 42,000 in 1989 to 62,000 in 1990 following the 4 June 1989 incident in Beijing. The number of emigrants leaving Hong Kong peaked at 66,000 in 1992 before moderating to a lower level following the tightening of quotas in major recipient countries like Canada and Australia (see Table 5.4).

In the 1990s a new trend of return migration emerged. Over the last few decades there have always been Hong Kong residents who emigrated abroad and return-migrated after obtaining foreign passports or residence status. Return migration abruptly gathered steam in 1992. It is the major reason behind the sharp increase in the balance of arrivals and departures, which reached 47,000 in 1992,

Table 5.5
Growth of Population and Labour Force

Year	Estimated Population (mid-year)	Populaton Growth Rate (%)	Labour Force (in million)	Labour Force Growth Rate (%)
1961	3,168,100	n.a.	n.a.	n.a.
1962	3,305,200	4.3	n.a.	n.a.
1963	3,420,900	3.5	n.a.	n.a.
1964	3,504,600	2.4	n.a.	n.a.
1965	3,597,900	2.7	n.a.	n.a.
1966	3,629,900	0.9	n.a.	n.a.
1967	3,722,800	2.6	n.a.	n.a.
1968	3,802,700	2.1	n.a.	n.a.
1969	3,863,900	1.6	n.a.	n.a.
1970	3,959,000	2.5	n.a.	n.a.
1971	4,045,300	2.2	n.a.	n.a.
1972	4,123,600	1.9	n.a.	n.a.
1973	4,241,600	2.9	n.a.	n.a.
1974	4,377,800	3.2	n.a.	n.a.
1975	4,461,600	1.9	1,964,000	n.a.
1976	4,518,000	1.3	1,895,300	−3.50
1977	4,583,700	1.5	1,927,100	1.68
1978	4,667,500	1.8	2,021,300	4.89
1979	4,870,500	4.3	2,141,000	5.92
1980	5,024,400	3.2	2,323,400	8.52
1981	5,183,400	3.2	2,489,500	7.15
1982	5,264,500	1.6	2,498,100	0.35
1983	5,345,100	1.5	2,540,500	1.70
1984	5,397,900	1.0	2,606,200	2.59
1985	5,456,200	1.1	2,626,900	0.79
1986	5,516,300	1.1	2,699,700	2.77
1987	5,572,400	1.0	2,728,200	1.06
1988	5,609,800	0.7	2,762,800	1.27
1989	5,638,500	0.5	2,752,800	−0.36
1990	5,649,800	0.2	2,748,100	−0.17
1991	5,690,800	0.7	2,798,800	1.84
1992	5,746,800	1.0	2,793,000	−0.21
1993	5,860,200	2.0	2,873,000	2.86
1994	6,007,900	2.5	2,972,600	3.47
1995	6,133,000	2.1	3,068,200	3.22
1996	6,311,000	2.9	3,093,800	0.83

Source: *Hong Kong Monthly Digest of Statistics.* Demographic Statistics Section, Census and Statistics Department; Immigration Department. Hong Kong.

84,000 in 1993, 87,000 in 1994, and 116,000 in 1995. These numbers are substantially higher than the corresponding figures (below 30,000) during most of the 1980s.

Information on return migrants is scant. The increase in the number of return migrants since 1992 may be related to the economic recession of major receiving countries of Hong Kong emigrants including the United States, Canada, and Australia. Hong Kong emigrants were attracted to return-migrate by the better economic opportunities available in Hong Kong. It is also possible that the number of return migrants has increased because the pool of former Hong Kong residents who are living overseas with foreign passports and who are therefore potential return migrants has expanded over time. The large balance of arrivals and departures in 1994 and 1995 could also be the result of a return flow of Hong Kong residents who worked in the Mainland. They returned to Hong Kong because of the economic downturn in the Mainland triggered by the tightening of macroeconomic control in 1994.

The demographic statistics collected by the Department of Census and Statistics do not allow us to identify the size of the flow of return migrants or to break down the components of the balance of arrivals and departures. Hence, it is difficult to be definitive about the reasons for the excessive volatility of the balance of arrivals and departures over time. What is important is that large fluctuations in the balance of arrivals and departures have caused substantial variability in the population growth rate in Hong Kong. In 1979 to 1980, before the abolition of the reached-base policy, the annual population growth rate in Hong Kong was as high as 3% to 4%, mainly because of the massive influx of illegal immigrants. After 1980 the rate fell dramatically throughout the decade to a low of 0.2% in 1990 on account of controlled immigration, declining fertility, and rising emigration. Since 1991 the increased flow of return migration has pushed the population growth rate upward to over 2% again. It reached 2.9% in 1996 (see Table 5.5).

Fluctuations in the population increase caused by volatility in the balance of arrivals and departures make population projections unreliable. Consequently, social policies that are driven by demographics, such as education, housing, social welfare, and transportation, are often thrown into disarray. For instance, based on the 1991 Census, the Department of Census and Statistics made several population projections for 1992 to 2011 in a report *Hong Kong Population Projections 1992–2011* published in May 1992. It projected that by mid-1999 the Hong Kong population would be 5,996,300, but in fact by mid-1994, only two years after the report was published, the population had grown to 6,007,900. Actual growth surpassed the 6 million mark five years ahead of the projection. The discrepancy in projection is largely due to the unexpected sudden surge in the balance of arrivals and departures, caused mainly by return migration.

To conclude, population growth in Hong Kong has been rather volatile over the last several decades. Before the abolition of the reached-base policy, the influx of illegal immigrants was the dominant factor that caused large fluctuations in population growth. Since the early 1980s, the uneven flow of emigrants and return migrants has been the principal cause. Fluctuations aside, Hong Kong's population growth has been underpinned by two steady sources of population increase, namely natural increase and legal immigration. It is significant that in recent years legal immigration has overtaken natural increase as the largest steady source of population increase in Hong Kong.

Immigration and Labour Supply

Throughout Hong Kong's history, there have been several major waves of Chinese immigrants; each wave boosted the population and hence the labour supply of Hong Kong. The influx of Chinese immigrants after the communist takeover of China supplied cheap labour for the early development of labour-intensive manufacturing industries in the 1950s. Each of the subsequent waves of immigrants sustained the development of labour-intensive industries until the mid-1980s.

Immigration has an immediate and a long-term effect on labour supply. The arrival of immigrants who participate in the labour market immediately adds to the labour force. The impact on the labour supply depends on the size of the flow of immigrants, the proportion of them that are economically active, their skills, and their educational background. The long-term and indirect effect is that immigration increases the population which ultimately determines the size of the labour force. In short, immigrants who are children and the children of immigrants will in due course enter the labour market and add to the labour supply.

Table 5.5 and Figure 5.1 show the close relationship between the rate of growth of the population and that of the labour force since 1975. A high labour-force growth rate is associated in the same year with a high population growth rate. This is a clear indication that an increase in the arrival of immigrants, return migrants, or expatriate workers in any year would immediately increase population growth and labour-force growth.

For instance, the last major influx of illegal immigrants from China following the opening up of China boosted the population growth rate from 1.8% in 1978 to 4.3% in 1979 and to 3.2% in 1980 and 1981. Over the same period, the labour force also grew at a fast rate, from 4.9% to 8.5%, which is substantially higher than the 1.7% growth rate of 1977. The population growth rate stayed below 2% from 1982 to 1992, when illegal immigration was halted and legal immigration from the Mainland was restricted by quota. During this period, the labour force in general also grew slowly, at a rate of 0% to 3%. In fact, its growth rate was negative in 1989, 1990, and 1992. Since 1993 the population growth rate has been above 2% again. This is on account of the large increase in the balance of arrivals and departures, which is mainly the result of return migration. Correspondingly, the labour-force growth rate increased from −0.2% in 1992 to over 3% in 1995, which is substantially higher than the growth rate for the decade of the 1980s after the abolition of the reached-base policy in 1980.

Figure 5.1
Rates of Growth of Population and Labour Force, 1976–96

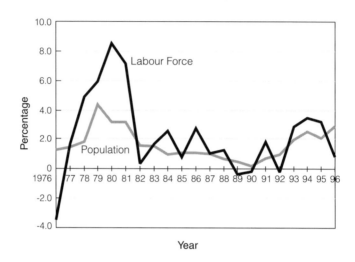

Year

Slow Growth of the Labour Force after the Abolition of the Reached-Base Policy

The importance of immigration to Hong Kong's labour supply is as evident in periods of low as in high immigration. Since the abolition of the reached-base policy in October 1980, illegal immigration has been largely contained, and a major source of labour for Hong Kong has been eliminated. Today some local employers may still defy the law and employ a certain number of illegal immigrants, but the number of illegal immigrants is small as compared to that in the pre-1980 period. Beginning in 1983 the Hong Kong government tightened control on immigration from China. Before that time, holders of two-way permits issued by the Chinese authorities who could return to China on those documents were allowed to take up residence in Hong Kong upon entry. In 1983 this policy was changed so that only holders of one-way permits were allowed to enter Hong Kong to take up residence. Legal immigration since 1983 was halved, from about 55,000 in 1980 to around 27,000 in 1983.

The reduction in the inflow of immigrants alone has caused a major slowdown of the growth of the labour force. From 1982 to the early 1990s the labour force grew at a slow pace of 0% to 2% in most years, and it actually shrank during a number of years. The effect of reduced immigration is exacerbated by four factors. These factors are natural increase, age structure, labour force participation, and emigration.

Declining Rate of Natural Population Increase

The decline in the rate of natural population increase has been discussed earlier. A sustained decline in this rate would slow down the growth of the labour force in the long run.

Changing Age Structure of the Population

Since the labour force is mainly drawn from the working-age population (15–64), a shift in the age composition will have a significant impact on the size of the labour force. The impact would be strong, in particular, where there is a shift from the younger to the older age bracket. To illustrate the shifting age composition, Table 5.6 shows the population size of two age groups. The 15–19 age group is the youngest group in the labour force and will provide manpower for the economy for many years to come. It shrank from 1.2 million in 1981 to about 886,000 in 1996. In contrast, the 55–64 age group, which is due to retire from the labour force, grew from about 410,000 to 513,000 over the same period. The combined effect of these demographic shifts across age groups is the reduction of the supply of labour over time.

Declining Labour Force Participation Rate

The male, the female, and the overall labour force participation rates have followed a similar pattern of decline since 1975. The fall was reversed in 1980 to 1981 because of the massive influx of young illegal immigrants from the Mainland who, by virtue of self-selection, were mostly potential labour force participants. The

Chapter 5

Table 5.6

Age Composition of Hong Kong Population, 1975–96

Year	Age 15–24	Age 55–64
1975	945,700	328,500
1976	975,100	338,900
1977	1,028,000	356,700
1978	1,059,300	370,200
1979	1,134,200	386,200
1980	1,165,800	397,800
1981	1,177,500	408,800
1982	1,153,700	421,000
1983	1,124,200	433,700
1984	1,087,100	445,400
1985	1,052,000	457,700
1986	1,023,200	469,600
1987	986,400	481,200
1988	950,700	491,200
1989	925,500	497,200
1990	896,100	499,600
1991	872,600	506,800
1992	849,500	509,400
1993	846,600	511,300
1994	860,800	512,600
1995	871,800	511,000
1996	886,400	512,900

Source: *Hong Kong Annual Digest of Statistics.*

general downward trend resumed in 1982 (see Table 5.7). This decline has reduced the labour supply over time.

The decline in the overall labour participation rate is mainly a result of the fall in the participation rate of the youngest and the oldest age groups in the labour force. The drop in the participation rates of youngsters (in the 15–19 and 20–24 age groups) is the result of the rapid expansion of secondary and tertiary education in Hong Kong in the 1980s. Increased educational opportunities caused many youngsters to defer entry into the labour force. As for workers in the 55–64 age group, the decline in their participation rate can be attributed to their earlier retirement. This is occurring because of

Table 5.7
Labour Force Participation Rates in Hong Kong, 1975–96

Year	Labour Force Participation Rates (%)		
	Male	Female	All
1975	82.8	47.6	65.9
1976	80.7	45.0	63.3
1977	79.7	43.9	62.2
1978	79.5	44.9	62.5
1979	79.4	43.8	62.0
1980	80.2	45.3	63.3
1981	82.5	49.0	66.3
1982	81.3	47.5	64.7
1983	80.9	47.4	64.5
1984	81.3	49.1	65.5
1985	80.4	48.5	64.8
1986	80.5	48.9	65.1
1987	80.2	48.6	64.8
1988	80.1	48.4	64.7
1989	79.5	47.3	63.7
1990	79.1	46.8	63.2
1991	78.8	47.8	63.4
1992	78.0	46.2	62.3
1993	78.1	46.5	62.5
1994	77.6	47.1	62.5
1995	77.3	48.0	62.8
1996	76.0	47.8	61.8

Source: Economics Database, Department of Economics, Chinese University of Hong Kong; *Hong Kong Monthly Digest of Statistics.*

the income effect. Many older employees who have had many years of sustained rises in real wage now want to quit and enjoy more leisure.

Rising Outflow of Emigrants

From 1980 to 1986 there was a steady outflow of emigrants from Hong Kong. The outflow was 18,000 to 22,000 per year but it accelerated in 1987 and reached a high of 66,000 in 1992 (see Table 5.4). The three major destination countries of emigrants were

Canada, the United States, and Australia. These were followed by
Singapore, New Zealand, and other countries.

The emigration trend rose sharply in 1987 because of two factors: the number of individuals applying for emigration and the
intake quotas set by the destination countries. On the supply side, as
the 1997 issue emerged in the early 1980s Hong Kong people
became increasingly concerned about the political future of Hong
Kong. At first, before committing themselves to plans for emigration, most people adopted a wait-and-see attitude toward the
negotiations between Britain and China on the future of Hong
Kong. The outflow of emigrants remained steady in those years.
The Sino-British Joint Declaration on the future of Hong Kong was
signed in 1984. The initial enthusiasm over the Joint Declaration
quickly gave way to scepticism and doubts. A surge of applications
for emigration began. The application process took about a year to
complete, so the increase in outflow was not visible until 1987.

On the demand side, two major destination countries, Canada
and the United States, changed their immigration policies and
quotas around 1987, thereby providing more opportunities for
Hong Kong applicants.

Emigrants are a selected and self-selected group. On the one
hand, they are selected by the destination countries as immigrants.
The selection criteria of two of the three major destination countries, Canada and Australia, are mainly based on point systems that
favour applicants who are young, well-educated, and English-
speaking; who are professionals, technicians, or managers by occupation; and who have the financial means of either supporting
themselves or starting a new business (if they are admitted under
business migration programmes) in the destination countries. On
the other hand, individuals self select themselves to apply for emigration. According to the human capital theory, individuals who
are young, who are adaptive to a new culture, and who are interna-
tionally employable because they possess skills and qualifications
that are transferable to other countries are more likely to migrate
(Sjaastad, 1962). Based on these two considerations, it is not sur-
prising that emigrants from Hong Kong are more likely than the

Table 5.8
Characteristics of Emigrants Compared to Those of the Hong Kong Population

Characteristics	Emigrants (1989)		Population (1991)
Age Group			
0–24	13,900	(33.1%)	36.5%
25–34	11,300	(26.9%)	21.1%
35–44	9,200	(21.9%)	16.0%
45–54	3,600	(8.6%)	8.8%
55–64	2,600	(6.2%)	8.9%
65 and above	1,400	(3.3%)	8.7%
Total	42,000	(100%)	100%
Occupation			
Professional, technical, administrative, and managerial	9,800	(23.3%)	11.7%
Other workers	13,000	(31.0%)	39.8%
Economically inactive	19,200	(45.7%)	51.5%
Total	42,000	(100%)	100%
Education			
First degree / postgraduate	6,100	(14.5%)	4.5%
Post-secondary	4,100	(9.8%)	4.2%
Matriculation (F6–F7)	2,500	(5.9%)	3.9%
Secondary (F1–F5)	18,900	(45.0%)	40.1%
Primary and below	10,400	(24.8%)	47.3%
Total	42,000	(100%)	100%

Source: Government Secretariat, *General Household Survey* 1989 and 1991 Census.
Note: The percentages for the emigrants are figures for 1989. The percentages for the population are figures from the 1991 Census.

general population to be in the 25–44 age group, to hold an academic degree, and to be employed as a professional, administrator, or manager (see Table 5.8). The rising outflow of emigrants had a detrimental effect on both the quality and quantity of the labour force in Hong Kong in the late 1980s and the early 1990s.

Labour Shortage and Inflation in Hong Kong, 1987–94

The slow growth of the labour force resulting from reduced immigration and other factors discussed above culminated in a labour

Chapter 5

Table 5.9
GDP Growth, Inflation and Unemployment, 1967–96

Year	GDP Growth Rate (%)	Inflation Rate (%) CPI (A)	Hang Seng CPI	Unemployment Rate (%)
1967	1.70	6.81	n.a.	n.a.
1968	3.33	2.84	n.a.	n.a.
1969	11.29	3.72	n.a.	n.a.
1970	9.18	7.88	n.a.	n.a.
1971	7.08	3.17	n.a.	n.a.
1972	10.33	6.60	n.a.	n.a.
1973	12.36	19.09	n.a.	n.a.
1974	2.33	14.84	n.a.	n.a.
1975	0.33	2.71	0.96	9.0
1976	16.23	3.42	4.19	5.1
1977	11.73	5.86	5.11	4.2
1978	8.50	5.92	5.63	2.8
1979	11.52	11.64	12.55	2.9
1980	10.12	15.53	14.81	3.8
1981	9.19	14.08	14.48	3.9
1982	2.75	10.53	10.05	3.6
1983	5.69	9.89	10.37	4.5
1984	9.97	8.18	9.04	3.9
1985	0.43	3.17	3.95	3.2
1986	10.77	2.92	4.80	2.8
1987	12.96	5.49	6.42	1.7
1988	7.97	7.41	8.72	1.4
1989	2.56	10.13	10.87	1.1
1990	3.40	9.73	11.28	1.3
1991	5.06	11.60	10.83	1.8
1992	6.26	9.35	9.74	2.0
1993	6.13	8.54	9.51	2.0
1994	5.29	8.10	10.00	1.9
1995	4.68	8.71	9.56	3.2
1996	4.74	6.01	7.03	2.8

Source: *Hong Kong Monthly Digest of Statistics.*

shortage from 1987 to 1994. The shortage first emerged as a problem in 1987 amidst an economic boom. It became more acute in 1988. The economic slowdown that began in 1989 and continued until 1990 did little to alleviate the shortage problem.

Table 5.10
Vacancy Rates, 1985–90
(%)

Economic Sector	1985	1986	1987	1988	1989	1990
Manufacturing	1.75	2.89	4.59	5.83	4.37	4.77
Wholesale, retail, import / export, restaurants, and hotels	0.91	1.72	3.53	4.38	3.38	4.32
Transport, storage, and communication	0.60	0.97	2.09	3.12	3.38	3.66
Financing, insurance, real estate, and business services	1.28	1.67	3.14	4.32	3.96	3.99

Source: *Hong Kong Annual Digest of Statistics* (fourth quarter figures).

The labour shortage manifested itself in a declining unemployment rate which fell below 2% beginning in 1987, the lowest since annual unemployment statistics began to be collected in 1975. It fell further to 1.1% in 1989 and remained below 2% until 1995 (see Table 5.9).

Other manifestations of the labour shortage were rising vacancy rates and rapidly increasing nominal and real wages across different sectors of the economy. Table 5.10 shows that job vacancy rates in the various sectors were very low in 1985, a year of recession. They began to rise in 1986 as the economy recovered. The increase in vacancy rates across all sectors was substantial in 1987. The pressure of the demand for labour was so strong in that year that employers found it difficult to retain workers and to recruit new workers to fill vacancies. Vacancy rates increased further in 1988. They fell slightly in 1989 following the slowdown in the economy but rose again in 1990. Throughout this period, all industries were affected by the shortage though to different extents. The worst affected industries were, in order of severity, metalworks, construction, retail, electrical appliances, electronics, printing, restaurants, and hotels.

Excess demand for labour also led to rapidly increasing nominal and real wages (see Table 5.11). The fall in real wages from 1983 to 1984 shown in Table 5.11 was the result of a massive influx

Chapter 5

Table 5.11

Growth Rate of Real Wages by Selected Major Economic Sectors, 1983–96

(%)

Year	Manufacturing	Trades, restaurants, and hotels, wholesale / retail, import / export	Business services	Construction
1983	−2.53	−4.07	−2.54	−6.0
1984	0.83	−0.66	1.72	−5.5
1985	2.89	1.74	4.67	0.9
1986	3.18	2.28	5.86	3.8
1987	3.08	4.21	2.85	15.4
1988	0.92	4.63	8.40	16.3
1989	1.70	3.33	7.43	11.5
1990	2.02	2.49	5.36	5.9
1991	−1.53	−1.71	1.75	n.a.
1992	0.23	4.31	−0.14	n.a.
1993	2.60	1.31	4.04	n.a.
1994	0.15	2.30	2.27	n.a.
1995	−2.59	−1.15	−1.85	n.a.
1996	0.70	−0.53	1.93	n.a.

Source: *Hong Kong Monthly Digest of Statistics.*

of immigrants from China from 1978 to 1980. Real wages began to increase rapidly from 1986 to 1987 as demand for labour increased with economic growth, rising much faster in some sectors than in others. Unlike in other sectors, real wage in manufacturing industries increased only moderately, because increasing outward-processing activities of Hong Kong manufacturers in China in the 1980s reduced the demand for local operatives and production workers. With the exception of manufacturing, increases in real wages in other sectors were substantial, notwithstanding the slow-down of the economy beginning in 1989. Increases in sectors like construction were staggering.

It is important to note that the labour shortage persisted throughout the entire business cycle, including during the period of economic slowdown from 1989 to 1990, when the GDP growth rate was as low as 2.56% and 3.40%, respectively. Indeed, there was full employment or even over-full employment during the economic slowdown. The answer to this vexing question lies in the stagnation of the growth of Hong Kong's labour force beginning in 1983. There was a strong demand for labour, in particular in the service sector, brought on by strong economic growth from 1986 to 1988 and by the restructuring of the economy of Hong Kong towards service industries following the opening up of China to foreign investment. This outstripped the labour supply, causing general labour shortages in the economy, with serious supply bottlenecks in specific sectors beginning in 1987. Indeed, the labour force expanded so marginally that despite the slowing down of the economy beginning in the second half of 1989, the labour market remained in disequilibrium. Until 1995, there were excess demand and labour shortages which persisted throughout the period of economic slowdown and beyond.

During the late 1980s, the growth in Hong Kong's capacity GDP was constrained by stagnation in the growth of the labour force. The fast-growing exogenous aggregate demand brought on by outward processing in South China ran up against the slow growing capacity GDP. This was the basic cause of the persistent high inflation in Hong Kong in the late 1980s and early 1990s. Sharp wage increases in the service sector fed directly into price increases of non-tradeables and services. Such increases were responsible for the high inflation rate in Hong Kong of 9% to 12% in the period 1989–92, a time when international prices for tradeables were relatively stable.

To summarize, stagnation in the growth of the labour force imposed a supply constraint on the economy and limited its productive capacity. The labour supply was so limited relative to demand that labour shortages persisted, and workers remained fully employed even during the period of the economic slowdown from 1989 to 1990. Economic restructuring and labour shortages generated large wage increases which kept the inflation rate high. As a result, the economy went through an unusual state of full employment with slow growth and high inflation from 1989 to 1990.

Policy Response to the Labour Shortage

To address the labour shortage problem of the late 1980s, the government realized that the labour supply had to increase. A number of factors that impinged on labour supply, such as fertility, demographic structure of the population, labour force participation, and emigration, were less amenable to government policy. The two sources of labour supply that could be more readily tapped by government policy initiatives were the importation of labour and the increase in immigrant intake.

In the late 1980s the Hong Kong government was preoccupied with the labour shortage problem, which was perceived to be a short-term phenomenon, but the government lost sight of the long-term problem of stagnation in the growth of the labour force. Consequently, it chose to address the labour supply problem through importing foreign labour.

The Hong Kong government had, and still has a long-standing policy of importing foreign workers, but this policy has hitherto been restrictive. In the past, only highly skilled technicians, professionals, and managers sponsored by their employers were issued employment visas. There is no quota restriction on such visas for foreigners to enter Hong Kong to work. The only exception to this restrictive policy has been the importation of domestic helpers.[1]

In response to pressure from industrialists and employer organizations that clamoured for extensive importation of labour to solve the labour shortage problem, the Hong Kong government decided to relax its formerly restrictive policy by widening the definition of skilled labour. In May 1989 the government announced a quota of 3,000 foreign workers and invited employers in the seventeen industries most affected by labour shortage to apply. Employers had to justify their need and show why they could not fill the jobs locally. Under this scheme, known as the General Scheme for Labour Importation, only "technicians and craftsmen" were to be approved for importation; semi-skilled and unskilled workers were not to be allowed entry. Employment contracts were to be for two years, and under normal circumstances they would not be renewable. Employers would be responsible for lodging and travelling costs of their imported workers. The proportion of imported workers in any company would be limited to not more than 20% of its workforce.

The scheme was extended in July 1990 when the Hong Kong government further relaxed the skill restrictions on importing foreign workers and set a quota of 14,700 for application with the following breakdown:

2,700	technicians, skilled workers,
10,000	experienced operatives, and
2,000	reserved quota assigned to construction workers for the airport and port development project.

Operatives are considered experienced if they have one year of work experience in the relevant field. For all practical purposes, with these new guidelines, the government opened the door for importing unskilled workers. It also abolished the requirement restricting imported workers to not more than 20% of a company's workforce. To protect local workers from possibly suffering a fall in wages as a result of competition from cheap imported labour, the government required that imported workers be paid the median wages of their job categories. The quota under the General Scheme on Importation of Labour was subsequently further expanded to 25,000 in 1991.

The quota set aside for construction workers for the new airport was soon raised to 5,500 when construction started in 1991. It was further raised to 17,000 in 1994 and subsequently to 27,000 at the peak of the airport construction in 1996.

The General Scheme for Labour Importation has been under continuous attack by labour unions and labour groups since its inception. The increase in the unemployment rate to over 3% in 1995 put pressure on the scheme. The government then decided not to fill the quotas vacated with foreign workers. By the end of 1996, excluding foreign workers in the airport project, only several thousand foreign workers under the General Scheme were still working in the territory. In February 1996 the General Scheme was replaced by the Supplementary Scheme for Labour Importation, with a quota of 2,000. This scheme was to be reviewed when the quota of 2,000 was fully allocated.

Policy Comparisons: Importation versus Immigration

Both the policy of importing foreign workers and that of increasing immigrant intake can increase labour supply. Each policy has its advantages and disadvantages. An analysis of the strengths and drawbacks of the two policies will assist us in deciding which policy to choose or whether a mix of the policies should be adopted.

The policy of importing labour has several advantages over the policy of increasing immigrant intake. First, skills that are in short supply can be specifically targeted rather easily in a labour-importation scheme, unlike in a scheme for increasing immigrant intake. This is especially so because Hong Kong has no control over the composition of immigrant intake. Under a labour-importation scheme, firms apply to import the workers that they want. Labour importation, therefore, is quicker and more effective than increasing immigration in terms of addressing specific labour bottlenecks. Second, under a labour-importation scheme, every person imported is an able-bodied worker who participates in the labour force to work full time or even overtime. In contrast, not every immigrant will become a member of the labour force. Some immigrants are home-makers or retired individuals. Moreover, immigrants usually bring their families. While their children will contribute to the labour force when they grow up, their spouses may not participate in the labour market at all. Hence, importing labour places less strain on the infrastructure and social services. Finally, importing labour can be adjusted flexibly to business cycles. If the economy goes into a recession, guest workers can be first repatriated to soften the impact of unemployment on the local labour force. This is precisely what happened in 1995 when the unemployment rate in Hong Kong rose above 3%.

The policy of increasing immigrant intake has several advantages over importing labour. Imported workers are typically unskilled or semi-skilled. Neither they nor their employers have any incentive to invest in training, given the short-term nature of their contracts. The value added per imported worker to production is relatively small. In contrast, immigrants do invest in further training. After settling in Hong Kong, some of them become highly skilled technicians and professionals, while others develop into entrepreneurs and industrialists (see Chapter 7). Indeed, many successful Hong Kong industrialists and entrepreneurs are immigrants from China. In short, the value added per immigrant is potentially much larger than that of an imported worker. Also, on a short-term basis, although importing workers with the right skills is theoretically an effective stopgap measure by which to relieve labour bottlenecks, in the long run immigration is more flexible in terms of addressing the long-term manpower needs of the economy. This is because immigration increases the population base forever. In the long run, working members of the population will always respond to economic incentives, which induce them to invest in human capital and take specific jobs. The labour market, using wage as a signal, will match workers of a certain skill with employers who demand that skill, thus solving the manpower problem. In contrast, identifying the right skill categories for labour importation is always difficult and contentious, as labour demand shifts continuously and the labour importation scheme is usually not flexible enough to cope with shifting demand. In addition, immigrants from the Mainland readily adapt and integrate into society, whereas imported workers tend to form enclave communities of their own. forming such communities can lead to social conflict, discrimination, and exploitation. Immigrants have a much stronger sense of belonging to their new home countries than guest workers who are sojourners. In terms of community building and identity, immigration is preferable to importing labour. Finally, since importation of labour is often targeted at specific occupations in which there is a perceived shortage of workers, it inevitably arouses the opposition of local labour groups. The policy is in nature politically divisive. In contrast, the impact of immigration on local workers is more diffuse and less specific to any occupation. It is politically more acceptable.

To conclude, importing labour is a short-term solution to the cyclical problem of supply bottlenecks in the labour market, whereas immigration is a long-term solution to the secular problem of slow growth in labour supply. In this chapter we have shown that the demographic factors that underpin the slow population growth and hence the labour force growth in Hong Kong are fundamental. The problem of slow growth in the labour force is a long-term one, and as such it should be addressed with a long-term policy of immigration. The issue of immigration as a means to increase the long-term labour supply will be revisited in Chapter 9, when we assess the immigration policy and make proposals for changes.

Note:

1. By 1996 there were a total of over 153,000 foreign domestic helpers working in Hong Kong, mostly from the Philippines.

CHAPTER 6

Economic Consequences of Immigration

Impact of Immigrants on Employment and Wages

One controversial immigration issue is that of the impact of immigrants on the labour market. Do immigrants compete with and displace natives workers? Does increased immigration cause unemployment? Do immigrants lower the wage of native workers? A common argument posed by labour unionists is that every immigrant who is employed displaces a native worker. This argument assumes that the number of jobs is fixed. In other words, it assumes that the inflow of immigrants has no impact on the scale of production. It also assumes that immigrants and native workers are perfect substitutes in production. Both assumptions are false, and the argument that follows from them is flawed.

At the other extreme, the alternative argument is that entry of immigrants into the labour market does not displace native workers, because immigrants take up jobs that native workers refuse to accept. The assumption is that the labour market is segmented into a primary sector of "good" jobs and a secondary sector of "bad" jobs (Piore, 1979). Native workers mostly work in the primary sector, while immigrants, especially those who are unskilled, are relegated to the secondary sector of "bad" jobs. This argument is also flawed because the presence of two sectors in a segmented labour market has been difficult to establish empirically.[1] If native workers refuse to take up "bad" jobs in the secondary sector, market competition will bid up the wage of those jobs until they are attractive to such workers (Borjas and Tienda, 1987).

Figure 6.1
Unskilled Labour Market

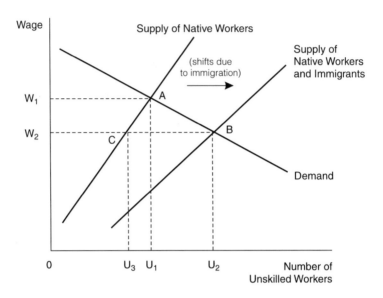

The impact of immigrants on the wage and employment of native workers depends critically on whether immigrants and native workers are substitutes or complements in production. Suppose immigrants are unskilled and are substitutes for unskilled native workers. Figure 6.1 shows the demand and supply of unskilled workers. Before the arrival of immigrants, the equilibrium wage and employment of unskilled native workers at A are W_1 and U_1 respectively. Immigration shifts the supply of unskilled workers outward. At the new equilibrium B, wage has gone down to W_2. Employment has increased to U_2 because firms that employ unskilled workers whose wage has gone down expand production. At the lower wage W_2, only U_3 native workers are willing to work (see point C). The employment of immigrant workers is $U_2 - U_3$; and together with the U_3 native workers, the total employment of unskilled workers becomes U_2. The number of unskilled native workers displaced is only $U_1 - U_3$, which is less than the number of immigrants employed $U_2 - U_3$. In other words, the employment of

Figure 6.2
Skilled Labour Market

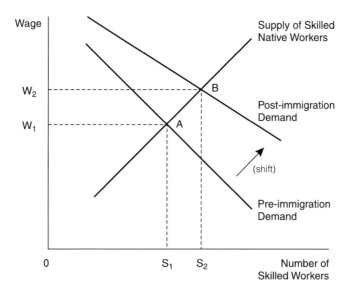

one immigrant worker does not displace one native worker because in the process total production and hence total employment have expanded. If the immigration process were reversed, and $U_2 - U_3$ immigrants were deported, the number of jobs created for native workers would be only $U_1 - U_3$, which would be less than the number of immigrants deported. To summarize, if immigrants and native workers are substitutes in production, immigrants will lower the wage and employment of native workers, but the displacement ratio will be lower than one for one.[2]

Now, consider the impact of immigrants on skilled native workers. Suppose immigrants are unskilled, and unskilled and skilled workers complement each other in production. The increase in unskilled immigrants will lower the wage of the unskilled workers and induce an expansion of production, which in turn will increase the demand for both unskilled and skilled workers. Figure 6.2 shows the shift in demand of skilled workers as a result of the lowering of the wage of unskilled workers because of immigration

Table 6.1

Elasticity of Native Wages with Respect to the Number of Immigrants in Locality (Wage / Earnings Studies)

Study	Impact of Immigrants on Wage / Earnings of:	Elasticity Estimate
Altonji and Card (1991)	Less Skilled Natives	+0.10
Bean, Lowell, and Taylor (1988)	Native Mexican Men	−0.005 to +0.05
	Black Men	−0.003 to +0.06
Borjas (1990)	White Native Men	−0.01
	Black Native Men	−0.02
Grossman (1982)	All Natives	−0.02
LaLonde and Topel (1991)	Young Black Natives	−0.06
	Young Hispanic Natives	−0.01
Altonji and Card (1991)	Immigrants	−0.40
Grossman (1982)	Immigrants	−0.23
Borjas (1986)	Immigrants	−0.92

Source: Various authors identified.

and the expansion of production. At the new equilibrium B, both the wage and employment of skilled native workers increase.

Reality lies somewhere between the two polar cases: (1) that both immigrants and native workers are being unskilled and substitutes, and (2) immigrants are unskilled but native workers being skilled with the two groups being complements. There are both unskilled and skilled workers among immigrants and native workers; perhaps the immigrants having a higher proportion of unskilled workers. The actual impact of immigrants on the labour market, therefore, is ambiguous and can only be ascertained empirically.

Borjas (1994) reports a number of studies on the effect of immigrants on the labour market of the United States. The methodology adopted by most of these studies involves comparing native earnings and the share of immigrants in the local labour market across localities in the United States. Table 6.1 summarizes the estimated elasticity of immigrants on wages or earnings of

Table 6.2

Elasticity of Native Employment with Respect to the Number of Immigrants in Locality (Unemployment Studies)

Study	Impact of Immigrants on Unemployment Rate of:	Elasticity Estimate
Muller and Espenshade (1985)	Black Natives	–0.010
Simon, Moore and Sullivan (1996)	Natives	+0.001
Winegarden and Khor (1991)	Young White Natives	+0.010
	Young Black Natives	+0.003

Source: Various authors identified.

natives and immigrants already in the United States. (Borjas, 1994). The elasticity measures the percent change in wages or earnings when the number of immigrants is increased by 1%.

The estimates show that the impact on native wages is very small. In an American city, a 10% increase in the number of immigrants (which is a sizeable increase) depresses native wages by about 0.2%. The impact on wages of immigrants who arrived earlier is much larger. A 10% increase in the number of immigrants lowers the wage of immigrants by 2% to 9%. The impact on immigrants is about ten times greater in magnitude than the impact on natives.

Similar estimates of the effect of immigration on the unemployment of natives also show a negligible effect. Table 6.2 illustrates that elasticity is in the 0.01 to –0.01 range. A 10% increase in immigrants results in at most a 0.1% increase in the unemployment of natives.

A study of a specific instance in which a large inflow of Cuban immigrants entered Miami in 1980 also shows that there was little impact on the local labour market. In April 1980 Fidel Castro declared that Cubans wishing to leave Cuba to move to the United States would be allowed to leave freely from the port of Mariel. By September 1980 about 125,000 Cubans, most unskilled, left for the United States. Miami's labour force grew suddenly by 7%, but Card

(1990) documents that there was a negligible impact on wage and employment in Miami between 1980 to 1985 as compared to other cities.

While studies on local labour markets seem to show that immigrants have had a negligible impact on wage and unemployment, a study on the economy-wide impact conducted by Borjas, Freeman, and Katz (1992) reveals a larger impact. They conclude that perhaps a third of the decline in the relative wage of American high school dropouts between 1980 and 1988 can be attributed to the inflow of less-skilled immigrants.

The difference between these findings could be the result of the fact that local labour markets in the United States are not closed economies (Borjas, 1994). Labour, capital and goods flow across regions and tend to equalize factor prices in the process, so that any impact of an inflow of immigrants is spread across regions within the country. Studies show that in localities where immigrants move in, there is a higher probability that native workers will move out, thus dissipating the depressive impact of immigrants on local wages (Filer, 1992; White and Hunter, 1993; Frey, 1994).

A similar study on the impact of immigration on wages in Hong Kong is by Suen (1994). Instead of comparing wages and the share of immigrants across metropolitan areas, as in studies of local labour markets in the United States, he compared them across age cohorts. This methodology presumably will avoid the dissipative effect caused by regional mobility of workers after immigration, since mobility across age cohorts is not possible. Suen (1994) estimates that the implied elasticity of immigrants on wages is –0.018, which is quite similar to the U.S. results. However, Suen's estimate of the impact of immigrants is also subject to the dissipative impact of labour mobility of a different sort. Even though mobility across age cohorts is impossible, the inflow of immigrants can cause the occupational mobility of natives. Specifically, unskilled immigrants of a certain age cohort could crowd into a low-paid occupation such as that of production worker or construction worker. This crowding might cause native workers in the same age cohort to respond by moving away from this occupation, thereby lessening the depressive impact of immigration on wage in that occupation. If mobility of native workers in the same age cohort into other occupations does not depress wages in those occupations much, the negative impact of immigration on wages in the age cohort concerned could be mitigated.

To summarize, in the equilibrium, when the effect of labour mobility and factor price equalization on wages work themselves out, the impact of an increase in the flow of immigrants, even though the flow may be sizeable, will be small. However, this does not preclude the possibility that the *initial* negative impact on wages could be significant if the inflow of immigrants were large, especially when the economy goes into a downturn. This assessment appears consistent with the Hong Kong data. The large influx of immigrants before the reached-base policy was abolished in 1980 depressed real wages in the early 1980s in industries such as manufacturing, wholesale, retail, import, export, restaurants and hotels, and construction (see Table 5.11), especially when the economy slowed down from 1982 to 1983 (see Table 5.9).[3] In construction, real wage experienced as much as a 6% fall in 1983. After a few years' time, the depressive impact of this large influx on wages had dissipated. Real wages rose strongly as the labour shortage became a problem in the latter half of the 1980s. In particular, construction real wage rose by as much as 16.3% and 11.5% in 1988 and 1989, respectively. Conversely, since 1993 the large increase in the flow of return migrants and legal immigrants from the mainland has boosted the rate of growth in the labour force in Hong Kong. This high rate of labour force growth together with the slowdown in the economy from 1995 to 1996 are the underlying factors behind weak and negative growth in real wages from 1995 to 1996.

Economic Benefits of Immigration

Before assessing an immigration policy, we need to evaluate the economic benefits that immigrants bring to the economy and to determine who gains and who loses as a result of the policy. There are many dimensions of economic benefits immigration may bring.

Chapter 6

Figure 6.3
Labour Market with Immigration Surplus

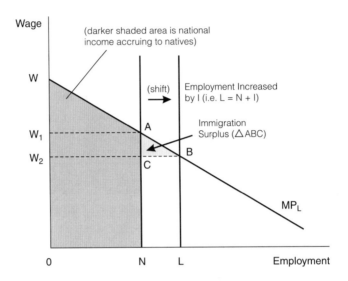

These may include a larger labour supply, a greater variety of skills available to the labour market, a larger output, an increase in the number of consumers in the economy, and a lowering of the price level as more products are produced. However, the most important single measure of economic benefits is whether immigration increases the national income — in particular, the national income of the native-born population.

For the purpose of illustration, let us assume a simple economy with only capital and labour as inputs. There is no skill differentiation between natives and immigrants. All workers are perfect substitutes in production. For simplicity, we also assume that the supplies of capital, and of both native-born labour and foreign labour, are perfectly inelastic. The production technology of the economy is constant returns to scale so that the entire output is distributed to the owners of capital and to workers. We assume that only natives own capital; immigrants do not bring capital with them.[4]

Figure 6.3 shows the equilibrium of the labour market before and after immigration. The labour demand curve is given by the marginal product of labour curve MP_L. The area under the marginal product of labour curve is the economy's total output, which is the national income. Initially, before immigration, the labour market equilibrium is at A. The national income accruing to natives is given by the area OWAN. After immigration, the inelastic labour supply curve moves outward by I, yielding a new equilibrium at B. The new output and hence the national income is the area OWBL. The increase in total output and national income due to immigration is the area NABL. Part of this national income is distributed to immigrants as labour earnings W_2I. The remaining portion of the increase in national income, called the immigration surplus and given by the area of the triangle ABC, accrues to the natives. Because immigrant workers are paid at their marginal product, they increase national income by more than what it costs to employ them, and this surplus goes to the native-born population as a whole, which benefits from the presence of immigrants. Note that native workers receive the lower wage W_2 after the inflow of immigrants. Their losses, however, are more than offset by the increase in income accruing to the capital owners through a higher rental price for capital (for an analysis see Borjas, 1995). The total output and hence the national income of the economy increases, but there is redistribution from native workers to capital owners.

The above analysis of economic benefits is a simplified one, as it is based on a simple economy of one type of labour with no skill differentiation and in which native and immigrant workers are perfect substitutes. To lend the analysis more realism, we should at least allow two types of native workers, those for whom immigrant workers substitute and those whom immigrant workers complement in production. It would be then clear from the model that both capital owners and native workers who are complementary to immigrant workers will gain, whereas native workers who are substitutes will lose as a result of increased immigration. Immigrant workers themselves in general gain from immigration, because immigration is a self-selection process.[5]

Table 6.3
Immigrant Participation in Welfare in the United States, 1970, 1980, 1990

Households with Immigrants	1970	1980	1990
Percentage of households with immigrant heads	6.8	7.6	8.4
Percentage of households with immigrant heads in population of households receiving public assistance	6.7	8.3	10.1
Percentage of public assistance income distributed to households with immigrant heads	6.7	9.1	13.1

Source: Borjas (1994)

Unskilled workers are likely to be substitutes for each other, but unskilled and skilled workers are complementary in production. Specifically, if immigrants are mostly unskilled, then an increase in the inflow of immigrants will hurt unskilled native workers but will benefit skilled native workers. The impact on unskilled native workers will depend on the depressive effect on the unskilled wage. As is discussed earlier, past experience in Hong Kong seems to indicate that a large increase in immigration will initially have an impact on wages, which will then dissipate within a few years. At equilibrium, the impact is negligible. Conversely, if immigrants are mostly skilled, skilled native workers will lose because of the substitution, but unskilled native workers will actually gain. In either case, owners of capital will gain, as the wage of either skilled or unskilled labour will be lower because of increased immigration.

Immigration and Welfare Cost

There has been considerable debate in countries that receive a large number of immigrants over whether immigrants should be entitled to the same level of social welfare as natives are and whether they pay enough taxes for their way in society. These debates are often political and passionate; they have been uninformed by research because studies on them have been sketchy.

In the United States, Blau's early work (1984) indicates that immigrant households have about the same probability of participating in public assistance programmes as native households have.

However, in 1965 a change in the U.S. immigration policy, which repealed national origin restrictions and made family ties the key criterion for admission, caused a shift in the ethnic composition and socioeconomic background of immigrants admitted into the United States in the last three decades.

Table 6.3 shows that there has been a significant shift in the participation rate of immigrant households in public assistance programmes in the United States over time as the background of immigrant cohorts changed (Borjas, 1994). In 1970, 6.8% all U.S. households were headed by immigrant, but only 6.7% of all households receiving public assistance had immigrant heads, so that immigrants were slightly under-represented among welfare households. However, by 1990 welfare participation of immigrant households had increased substantially. The share of immigrant households in the population had increased to 8.4%, but their share among all households receiving public assistance had increased further to 10.1%. Immigrant households became over-represented among welfare households. The percentage of public assistance income distributed to immigrant households was also disproportionately high, at 13.1%.

In the United States in recent years, as compared to earlier decades, not only are immigrant households more likely to be on welfare, on average they also receive larger welfare payments than native households do. There is also evidence that the welfare participation rate of an immigrant cohort tends to increase over time instead of decreasing, as one would expect it to do if the immigrants had adapted and assimilated into the economy. Borjas (1994) reports that 5.5% of the households that arrived between 1965 and 1969 received public assistance in 1970, but the percentage increased to 10% in both 1980 and 1990. This may be because, the longer that immigrants stay in the U.S., the more they learn about their eligibility and the application details of welfare programmes. The more generous the welfare programmes, the more likely that the economic costs and welfare burden of increasing immigration will outweigh the economic benefits it brings.

In contrast to the situation in the United States, Baker and Benjamin (1993) find that immigrants in Canada have a lower probability of being welfare recipients than natives do. There are very few other country studies that document the welfare participation of immigrants. In Hong Kong there is no reliable information on welfare participation of immigrant households. Immigrants are eligible to receive welfare benefits after one year of residence in Hong Kong. The benefits involved are much lower in terms of both variety and amount than the welfare benefits in the United States or Canada. However, if the U.S. experience is any guide, a change in Hong Kong's immigration selection criteria that favours family reunion by the Chinese authorities will increase the intake of economically inactive immigrants in Hong Kong. Such people are more likely to become welfare recipients after immigration. The Chinese authorities' issuance of one-way permits to Mainland-born children of Hong Kong permanent residents separately from their mothers also increases welfare dependency in Hong Kong. Children coming to Hong Kong to join their fathers without their mothers create child-care problems for the working fathers. There have been reported incidences of these fathers quitting their jobs to stay home in order to care for their children; these families rely on public assistance for financial support.

Immigration and Cost of Public Goods Provision

Another controversial issue is that of whether immigrants pay enough taxes to cover the public services they receive. For the host country not to be worse off in terms of public expenditure after receiving immigrants, the total amount of taxes paid by immigrants must be sufficient to pay for both their public assistance benefits as well as for increases in spending on the public services they enjoy. Research in this area is even more sketchy than the research done on welfare participation by immigrants.

On the theoretical side, we know that if the government provides only *pure* public goods, then immigration will not affect public expenditure. However, most public goods provided by the government are not pure. For instance, immigrants may increase congestion in the use of such public goods provided by government as hospitals, schools, parks, roads, and service by civil servants. The marginal cost of providing these public goods to immigrants is not zero. In other words, an increase in the number of immigrants causes congestion and lowers the degree of use of these public goods by the native-born population. To relieve the congestion, the government has to spend more in order to provide more of these goods.

Little research has been done on the cost structure in the provision of public goods. We do not know whether the marginal cost of providing these public goods is less than, equal to, or greater than the average cost. For argument's sake, let us first suppose that the marginal cost of public goods provision is equal to the average cost and that the per capita income of the immigrant population is the same as that of the native-born population. Then the taxes paid by an average immigrant are the same as the taxes paid by an average native, which contribute toward the public expenditure for public goods provision. If this is the case, the taxes contributed by an average immigrant will pay for the public services he or she enjoys in the same way and to the same extent as an average native. Empirically, however, we know that on average, immigrants' income is lower than natives'. Therefore, the average immigrant will pay less taxes than will the average native. If immigrants are to pay their way in terms of the use of public goods to the same extent as natives do, the marginal cost of public goods provision will have to be less than the average cost. In other words, if it costs less to provide public services to immigrants at the margin than at the average, immigrants could pay their way even though they have lower incomes and pay less taxes.

It is difficult to be more precise in the absence of more research on the cost structure of public goods provision. It is likely that many public goods enjoyed by immigrants have a lower-than-average marginal cost of production. Whether immigrants pay their way in taxes also depends on the magnitude of transfer payments in the form of public assistance to which they are entitled. The more generous the welfare entitlements, the more likely that immigration will impose a tax burden on the native-born population.

Although no in-depth research has been conducted on the tax issues and problems of welfare dependency in Hong Kong, some qualitative observations on the public goods and welfare benefits provided for immigrants would be useful to our assessment of Hong Kong's immigration policy. The major transfer payment that immigrants can receive is the Comprehensive Social Security Assistance (CSSA), for which new immigrants are eligible after one year of residence in Hong Kong.

As regards public goods, the most important one in terms of benefits is public rental housing. Due to the nature of the use, the marginal cost of providing public rental housing to an immigrant family is close to if not equal to the average cost. At present, to be eligible for public housing, at least half of the family members in the household must have resided in Hong Kong for at least seven years. The period of eligibility for public housing is longer than the period for public assistance. This is appropriate in view of the fact that the cost of providing public housing is by itself high, and the marginal cost of provision in this case is close to the average cost.

In general *as a whole*, natives who live in public housing have been paying taxes (although many individuals may not be taxpayers) for a certain number of years. Immigrants *as a whole* should also have been taxpayers for a number of years (even though individual immigrants may not be taxpayers) before they become eligible for public housing. This way, they will be paying their way in the same way and to about the same extent as the native-born population. Public rental housing is heavily subsidized. As groups, natives and immigrants residing in public housing pay for less than the marginal cost of public housing provision. Government subsidization notwithstanding, the important point is that there should be parity between the extent to which each of the two groups is paying for public housing through taxes. To achieve some sort of parity, the period that immigrants must meet to be eligible for public housing should not be too short in view of the high cost of provision;

otherwise immigrants will be favoured over natives. Without a detailed analysis of the cost structure of public housing provision and of the profile of tax payments among native residents in public housing, it is not possible to be precise about the parity or the period. However, it appears that shortening the eligibility period to less than seven years would likely create a bias in favour of immigrants over natives.

Another important and costly public good is education. This good is particularly relevant to immigrant children. The marginal cost of schooling provision for immigrants is also close to the average cost when the education system is operating at full capacity. However, schooling is quite different from housing because it is not purely a consumption; it is also an investment. Even though the cost of provision is high, it is more like an investment cost. All analyses on the rates of return to public and private schooling investments in Hong Kong show that the returns are quite high (Lam and Liu, 1997). In other words, public spending on schooling of immigrant children brings significant returns to the individuals concerned and to society. Therefore, there should be no restriction on the eligibility of immigrant children for publicly funded places in schools.

Other public goods that immigrants enjoy in Hong Kong include hospitals, roads, parks and public services. The marginal costs of providing for the immigrants are relatively minor compared to housing and education. Another characteristics of these goods is that restriction on their use is infeasible. In general, there should be no period of eligibility imposed on the immigrants for the use of these public goods.

Notes

1. For a critical review, see Cain (1976).

2. A simple analysis of a single factor market is given by Ehrenberg and Smith (1991). For a more complex analysis involving more factors, factor equalization, and capital mobility, see Greenwood and McDowell (1986), Simon (1989), and Friedberg and Hunt (1995).

3. Unfortunately we have no information on real wage prior to 1983, especially for the period 1979–81, when the large influx of illegal immigrants came to Hong Kong, to buttress our assessment that a sizeable inflow of immigrants into Hong Kong could initially depress real wage.

4. This analysis is based on Borjas (1995).

5. Here we consider only the economic benefits of immigration. Neither other social benefits arising from family reunion nor the political benefits of immigration are considered. If there had been no economic gains in immigration, immigrants would not have migrated. Those who migrated but found that they do not benefit economically from the move would have return migrated.

CHAPTER 7

Economic Performance of Immigrants in Hong Kong

Economic Assimilation

In this chapter we analyze the economic performance of immigrants after arrival in Hong Kong, as measured by their earnings.[1] Specifically, we analyze the economic assimilation of immigrants. After immigrants arrive in the receiving country, they gradually assimilate and integrate into the community. Assimilation takes place at work, in the neighbourhood, and at school. The assimilation process can take place at the economic, social, and cultural levels. In this book we are concerned only with economic assimilation.

Narrowly defined, economic assimilation describes a process whereby an immigrant who stays longer in the receiving country earns more than an equivalent immigrant who stays for a shorter time. At the time of arrival, immigrants earn less than natives, because they do not have country-specific skills for the labour market of the receiving country. It has been argued that new immigrants rapidly accumulate these skills after arrival, such as language and cultural know-how. Since immigrants are a self-selected group, they are more able and motivated than natives (Chiswick, 1978), and hence they accumulate more specific human capital than the natives. Thus, the earnings of immigrants rise rapidly after arrival and eventually equal or even exceed the earnings of natives possessing the same observed human capital characteristics. Chiswick (1978) estimates that it takes ten to fifteen years for a typical immigrant to overtake a typical native in earnings in the United States.

101

Borjas (1985, 1994, 1995) challenges the interpretation of the positive correlation between relative earnings and years since immigration (on the basis of cross-sectional data) as evidence of assimilation. He argues that because of a change in the U.S. immigration policy, recent cohorts of immigrants are of a different quality than those who arrived twenty or thirty years ago. Earlier cohorts earn more because their skill level is higher on average, not because of assimilation. Borjas (1994, 1995) takes a broader view, suggesting that assimilation describes the process of convergence of earnings of an arrival cohort of immigrants with the earnings of natives. The observed human capital characteristics of immigrants and natives are not held fixed in this calculation. Borjas (1994, 1995) adjusted for the cohort effects and other effects and concludes that assimilation in the narrow sense is much less than that implied by cross-sectional earnings comparisons. Another conclusion is that assimilation in the broad sense of earnings convergence is also rather weak, because the quality of newly arrived immigrant cohorts has deteriorated over time to such an extent that the earnings gap between the more *recent* arrival cohorts of immigrants and natives has widened in comparison to the gap between natives and *earlier* cohorts.

The finding of Borjas (1985) is disputed by LaLonde and Topel (1992) who find strong evidence of assimilation as it is narrowly defined. Holding education and experience constant, they estimate that the rate of assimilation for most ethnic groups is over 2% (increase in earnings capacity) a year in the first ten years of experience in the U.S. labour market. They also dispute Borjas's claim that immigrant quality declines within ethnic groups; they find little evidence for the claim. Immigrant quality, however, did decline overall, largely as a result of changes in the ethnic composition of new immigrants in the United States.

Bloom and Gunderson (1991) provide evidence of a moderate assimilation effect for immigrants in the Canadian labour market, suggesting that immigrants take thirteen to twenty-two years to catch up with natives in terms of wage. They also show that the unobserved quality of immigrants declined as a result of changes in

Canada's immigration policy that had led to a sharp increase in the proportion of immigrants admitted on the basis of family ties. In a more recent study, Bloom, Grenier, and Gunderson (1994) show that recent immigrant cohorts have had more difficulty assimilating into the Canadian labour market than earlier ones. The reasons were: recent changes in the Canadian immigration policy, labour market discrimination, and a prolonged recession in the early 1980s.

Their findings are disputed by Baker and Benjamin (1994) who find very little assimilation for most immigrant cohorts in Canada. They find evidence that earlier cohorts enjoy a moderate rate of assimilation, but their measure is imprecisely estimated and is sensitive to the base group used to control for intercensal earnings growth. There is substantial evidence that the labour market outcomes of successive immigrant cohorts are declining over time. Many arrival cohorts experience no earnings growth or even experience divergence in earnings relative to natives.

In a study on immigrants in Germany, Dustmann (1993) argues that there might not be positive self-selection if migrants are temporary and therefore have less incentive to invest in receiving country-specific human capital after migration. He shows that temporary migrants in Germany who come mainly from southern Europe and Turkey do not close their earnings gap with respect to natives as their stay in Germany lengthens.

Studies on various other countries yield mixed results on whether there is economic assimilation of immigrants. In this chapter we analyze economic assimilation of immigrants in Hong Kong using the 1981 and 1996 census data of Hong Kong. We find that instead of convergence, there has been divergence in the earnings of Chinese immigrants in Hong Kong with respect to native earnings. The divergence is mainly caused by the intercensal deterioration in the relative prices of observed skills of immigrants. Immigrants have been assimilating in the narrow sense at a rate similar to that of other countries, but this effect is overwhelmed by the change in relative rates of return to schooling of immigrants; that change has caused the divergence.

Table 7.1
Earnings Gap between Immigrants and Male Native Employees,
Hong Kong, 1981 and 1996

Earnings Gap between Natives and:	1981	1996
All immigrants	–0.1128	–0.2868
Pre-1981 Arrival Cohort	–0.1128	–0.2864

Source: Hong Kong Census 1981 and By-census 1996. Sample dataset.

Note: The figures represent the earnings gap, expressed as the "mean log earnings differential"; negative means immigrants earn less than natives.

Immigrants vs Natives: Divergence in Earnings and Rates of Return to Schooling

In both the 1981 and 1996 censuses in Hong Kong, immigrants can be identified by their place of birth. The 1981 Census reports the year of arrival only of immigrants who arrived within five years of the census, while the 1996 Census reports year of arrival of immigrants. This allows us to trace the economic performance of a synthetic immigrant cohort of pre-1981 arrivals in both repeated cross-sections over a period of fifteen years. We will focus on the analysis of the assimilation of this cohort. A finer breakdown of this cohort by year of arrival is not possible because of data limitation in the censuses.

The sample for analysis consists of male employees aged twenty to sixty-four. Relative earnings of male immigrant employees are measured by the difference in mean log earnings between immigrants and natives. Two stylized facts are apparent from the data shown in Table 7.1. First, immigrants earned on average less than natives did. Second, the relative earnings of the pre-1981 arrival cohort declined over time from 1981 to 1996. Instead of earnings convergence between immigrants and natives, there was divergence. Specifically, the earnings gap between immigrants of this cohort and natives widened from 11.3% in 1981 to 28.6% in 1996 (subject to the log approximation).

The change in relative earnings could be the result of a combination of several factors, including a change in relative endowment of observed human capital characteristics between immigrants and natives, a change in relative prices of these characteristics, assimilation (in the narrow sense) over the fifteen-year period, and a change in the wage structure that affects different skill groups unequally.

To help us understand the change in relative earnings of immigrants over time, a standard Mincerian earnings function relating log earnings to years of schooling, years of work experience, and its squared term is estimated for natives and the pre-1981 arrival cohort of immigrants separately at two points in time, 1981 and 1996. Estimates of the coefficients of the earnings regressions are shown in Appendix A.

Both the schooling and the experience coefficients of immigrants are significantly lower than the corresponding coefficients of natives. The schooling coefficient can be interpreted as the rate of return to schooling — in other words, the proportionate increase in earnings as a result of one extra year of schooling. Table 7.2 shows that the rate of return to schooling of natives in 1981 was 0.0954; in other words, there was a 9.54% increase in earnings for each extra year of schooling. This rose substantially to 11.31% in 1996. The rate of return to schooling of immigrants in 1981 was much lower, at 4.57%, which increased to 5.94% in 1996. As a result, the differential in the rate of return to schooling between immigrants and natives widened from –4.97% in 1981 to –5.37% in 1996, an increase of 0.4 percentage points. The differential in experience coefficient between the two population groups also increased somewhat over the same period. We will show in the following section that the divergence in earnings between natives and immigrants in the period 1981–96 can be largely accounted for by the divergence in their rates of return to schooling and the experience coefficients.

Earnings Divergence: A Decomposition

The relative earnings of immigrants and their intercensal change can be decomposed into a number of components.[2] Table 7.3

Chapter 7

Table 7.2

**Rates of Return to Schooling of Hong Kong Natives and Immigrants
(Pre-1981 Arrival Cohort), 1981 and 1996**

	1981	1996
Rate of Return to Schooling		
Natives	0.0954	0.1131
Immigrants	0.0457	0.0594
Immigrants / Natives Differential	−0.0497	−0.0537
Experience Coefficient		
Natives	0.0680	0.0569
Immigrants	0.0345	0.0200
Immigrants / Natives Differential	−0.0335	−0.0369

Table 7.3

**Decomposition of Earnings of Immigrants (Pre-1981 Arrival Cohort)
Relative to Those of Natives, 1981–96**

Components	1981	1996	Change 96–81
Price Effect	−0.4716	−1.0371	−0.5655
Quantity Effect	0.0466	−0.1435	−0.1901
Unobserved Effect	0.3122	0.8942	0.5820
Relative Earnings (Total)	−0.1128	−0.2864	−0.1736

Source: See Table 7.1

reports the decompose capital characteristics between immigrants
and natives, (2) the quantity effect (*endowment*) *attributable* to
differing human capital "quantities" between immigrants and
natives, and (3) the unobserved effect. The latter is the sum of the
assimilation effect and the residual effect, which in turn is made up
of the difference in the time effect on prices of unobserved skills and
the cohort effect.

It is clear from Table 7.3 that the major factor behind the low
relative earnings of immigrants in 1981 (−0.1128) and 1996
(−0.2864) is their low price effect, which is a result of the differential

in the rate of return to schooling and experience coefficients between immigrants and natives. In contrast, the quantity effect, which measures the quality of immigrants relative to natives, is small in magnitude. The difference in relative endowments ("quantity") of human capital between natives and immigrants is not an important factor.

More important, column 3 of Table 7.3 shows a substantial intercensal decline in relative earnings of immigrants of the pre-1981 arrival cohort. the amount of decline is 0.1736 (over seventeen percentage points). The major driving force behind this decline is the worsening price effect of immigrants (−0.5655) accounted for by the widening differential in the rate of return to schooling across the two censuses. The quantity effect of immigrants has also worsened somewhat (−0.1901), largely because the mean education attainment of natives has increased faster than that of immigrants. However, the magnitude of this effect is relatively small.

The change in the unobserved effect, 0.5820, from 1981 to 1996 in Table 7.3 is fifteen times the annual rate of assimilation calculated elsewhere.[3] Hence, the rate of assimilation as a result of the accumulation of receiving country-specific human capital by immigrants after arrival is 3.88% of earnings for every year of stay, suggesting that, *ceteris paribus*, it would take immigrants about twenty-six years to catch up with natives. The assimilation effect could have been estimated more directly and with greater precision had we possessed information on the year of arrival. Our indirectly estimated rate of assimilation is nevertheless in the same range as those of other studies.

To summarize, Chinese immigrants assimilated in the narrow sense into the Hong Kong labour market in the 1980s. The rate of assimilation was similar to that experienced by immigrants in other countries. However, over the same period, the wage structure changed, and the relative prices of observed skills moved against immigrants. Specifically, the relative rates of return to schooling of immigrants deteriorated; and this effect dominates the assimilation effect. As a result, there has been earnings divergence rather than convergence between immigrants and natives. Hence, even though there is assimilation in the narrow sense, in the broad sense, there is no assimilation.

Economic Restructuring and Divergence in Rates of Return to Schooling

It remains to be explained why rates of return to schooling and experience coefficients between immigrants and natives have diverged over time. One possible hypothesis is increasing labour market discrimination against immigrants from 1981 to 1996. This explanation, however, is not very plausible. Unlike immigrants in other countries, immigrants from the Mainland are ethnic Chinese, just like the native-born in Hong Kong. They share the same language and culture. As much as 28% of the population of Hong Kong in 1996 were immigrants, and almost all the native-born have parents or ancestors who are or were immigrants from the Mainland. The longer Chinese immigrants stay in Hong Kong, the more readily they integrate socially and culturally into the local community. Even if there had been labour market discrimination against new immigrants, staying longer in Hong Kong would have reduced it. After all, by 1996 all immigrants of the pre-1981 arrival cohort had been in Hong Kong for more than fifteen years.

An alternative hypothesis is to attribute the widening differential to the shifting demand for skills of different sources as the economy of Hong Kong restructured rapidly in the 1980s. Natives acquired all their schooling and work experience in Hong Kong, whereas immigrants acquired most of their schooling and part of their work experience in the Mainland. Like in most empirical studies on this subject, we could breakdown the schooling of immigrants into schooling acquired in the Mainland before immigration and schooling acquired after immigration in Hong Kong; but we cannot because of the limited data. Nevertheless, we can infer from the age distribution of immigrants on arrival that most new immigrants are likely to have completed their formal schooling before migration.[4] Furthermore, it has been reported that the participation rate of new immigrants in part-time continuing education after migration is very low.[5] Hence, it is safe to conclude that immigrants' reported schooling was mostly acquired in the Mainland before immigration to Hong Kong. It has been noted in the literature of immigration that the immigrant's rate of return to schooling acquired in the sending country is lower than that acquired in the receiving country after migration because of specificity of human capital (Lam, 1986). It is possible that the human capital of immigrants acquired through schooling and experience in the Mainland is not only initially less productive, but is also relatively less productive as the economy restructures.

The economy of Hong Kong restructured rapidly following the opening up of China in 1979. Hong Kong manufacturers took advantage of low labour and land costs in South China and moved their labour-intensive production operation across the border, leaving such front-end and back-end manufacturing processes as sourcing, merchandizing, marketing, and design in Hong Kong. These are the higher value-added processes that require different skills than those needed for assembly. Products of these outward-processing activities of Hong Kong manufacturers in the Mainland are mostly re-exported through Hong Kong. This stimulated rapid growth in the re-export trade in Hong Kong, and demand for services to support these activities expanded rapidly, including transportation, storage, business services, insurance, and trade financing. The Hong Kong economy rapidly restructured itself to become service oriented. What was unusual about the economic restructuring of Hong Kong in the 1980s was its speed. From 1981 to 1991 the share of manufacturing in employment fell from 41.3% to 28.2%. An index of sectoral shift in employment measuring the minimum proportion of workers who had to change sectors as a result of sectoral shift from 1987 to 1992 for Hong Kong is 8.9, as compared with 3.27 for Singapore, 6.5 for Korea, 2.22 for Japan, and 2.16 for the United States.[6]

As the economy restructures, the wage structure changes in favour of skills that are productive in high value-added manufacturing processes and in service industries. The human capital that natives possess, being acquired through schooling investments and work experience in Hong Kong, is probably flexible and adaptive to this shift in demand for skills. In contrast, the human capital acquired by immigrants in the Mainland through schooling and experience is probably productive in assembly processes but not in the high value-added processes of merchandizing, marketing, and design or in service industries. Examples in the latter include business services, insurance, finance, export, and import. Compared with the last decade, service industries in Hong Kong are now more interpersonal, skill-intensive, and international, requiring a high degree of language proficiency (especially knowledge of the English language). New jobs expect workers to possess more knowledge about the business, economic, and social environment of Hong Kong and the world. It is possible that education and work experience in the Mainland does not help immigrants acquire these skills easily; and this gives rise to the declining relative productivity, relative rates of return to schooling, and experience coefficients.

Immigrants and Entrepreneurship

The previous analysis has shown that, relative to natives on average, earlier immigrants have not been very successful in the labour market as employees. The reason is possibly the lack of the type of human capital investment that is productive in a service-oriented economy. The relatively poor economic returns that immigrants receive as employees provide the impetus for them to engage in alternative economic activities, for example becoming employers or self-employed.

Table 7.4 compares the percentages of recent and earlier immigrants among the economically active to their percentages among employers and the self-employed. In both 1981 and 1996, among employers and the self-employed, recent immigrants are under-represented compared with their shares among the economically active. For instance, in 1996, 2.8% of the economically active were recent immigrants, but among employers (self-employed), only 1.9% (1.1%) were recent immigrants. Conversely, new immigrants are slightly over-represented as employees. This pattern is to be expected, as new immigrants usually have neither the capital nor the networks necessary to start their businesses or practices within a few years of arrival in Hong Kong. It is more likely that they will first establish themselves by finding employment as employees.

However, as immigrants stay longer in Hong Kong and become "earlier" immigrants (in our classification), the pattern changes. The rapid obsolescence of the human capital they acquired in the Mainland and consequently the relatively low rate of return to their skills in their employment as employees have pushed some of them to consider alternatives, such as becoming employers or self-employed. The longer their stay in Hong Kong, the more likely they are to accumulate sufficient savings to start their own businesses. Furthermore, because of self-selection, immigrants are probably more prone to risk-taking than natives.

The combination of the push factor and the self-selection factor may explain why immigrants are, relatively speaking, more likely to be entrepreneurs than natives after immigrants have stayed in Hong Kong for a period of time. Table 7.4 shows that in 1981, 41.2% of the economically active were earlier immigrants, but they represented as many as 65.9% of all employers. On the other hand, natives made up 47.8% of the economically active but only 28.2% of the employers. The over-representation of earlier immigrants among the self-employed is even more prominent, especially among hawkers (66.6%). This pattern is essentially unchanged in 1996, except that the over-representation of earlier immigrants, and conversely the under-representation of natives, among both employers and the self-employed is lower. For reasons unknown, natives have become more entrepreneurial as employers or the self-employed in recent years than they were, say, two decades ago. This recent shift in balance notwithstanding, earlier immigrants are still relatively more likely to become entrepreneurs than natives.

Immigrants' performance as employees (measured by earnings) in general has not been as good as that of natives. Do immigrant entrepreneurs perform better? The performance of immigrants as entrepreneurs can also be measured by their relative mean income with respect to native entrepreneurs. Earlier, we show that the mean

Table 7.4

**Percentage of Natives and Immigrants as Employers,
Self-Employed, and Employees, 1981 and 1996**

Enumerated Population who were:	All Economically Active	Employer	Self-Employed	Employee	Hawker	All Others
1981						
Natives	47.8	28.2	24.8	20.0	28.4	50.3
Earlier Immigrants	41.2	65.9	70.1	74.8	66.6	37.8
Recent Immigrants	8.4	1.3	3.1	3.9	2.5	9.3
Others	2.6	4.6	2.0	1.3	2.5	2.6
Total	100.0	100.0	100.0	100.0	100.0	100.0
1996						
Natives	60.4	53.3	53.8	39.0	56.1	61.1
Earlier Immigrants	27.0	37.2	40.0	56.3	37.1	25.4
Recent Immigrants	2.8	1.9	1.1	0.9	1.2	2.9
Others	9.8	7.6	5.1	3.8	5.6	10.6
Total	100.0	100.0	100.0	100.0	100.0	100.0

Source: Hong Kong Census 1981 and By-census 1996. Sample dataset.

earnings of male immigrant employees diverge from those of male native employees (see Table 7.1). In other words, immigrant employees on average are falling farther behind their native counterparts. Table 7.5 shows the opposite trend between immigrant and native employers. In 1981 the mean income of earlier immigrant employers was about 14.1% lower than that of native employers. This gap remained virtually unchanged in 1996. The improvement in the mean income of recent immigrant employers is, however, substantial. Being disadvantaged in terms of capital, networks, and experience with the markets, recent immigrant employers earned 46.7% less than native employers did in 1981, but they narrowed the gap substantially in 1996, to 9.5%.

Recent immigrants in 1996 were probably better prepared to be entrepreneurs in Hong Kong than earlier cohorts of recent immigrants who arrived prior to 1981. The economic reform and the opening up of China to foreign investments in 1979 have facilitated

Table 7.5
Income Gaps between Immigrant / Native Employers and Self-Employed
1981 and 1996

	Earlier Immigrants		Recent Immigrants	
	1981	1996	1981	1996
Employer	–0.141	–0.142	–0.467	–0.095
Self-Employed	–0.042	–0.093	–0.143	–0.025

Source: See Table 7.4.

Note: Income Gaps are measured by the mean log income differentials.
A negative value means immigrants earn less than natives.

flow of information between Hong Kong and the Mainland which could not take place before. Immigrants of more recent cohorts, especially those from Guangdong, must have acquired considerable information about Hong Kong before immigration. They were exposed to a more market-oriented economy in the Mainland after the economic reform, and they had a better understanding of private business and how markets work before coming to Hong Kong. Moreover, the process of the issuance of one-way permits in the Mainland is so opaque and so prone to corruption that the implicit selection criteria favour applicants who are entrepreneurial in terms of securing one-way permits within the system. In contrast, earlier cohorts of immigrants who arrived in Hong Kong before the 1980s had been living for years in an isolated country with a centrally planned economy. They had little idea of how a free market and a capitalist economy work, and they had little knowledge about Hong Kong when they arrived. Compared with more recent cohorts of immigrants who arrived in the late 1980s, earlier cohorts were less prepared to participate in the economy of Hong Kong, either as employees or as employers.

Immigrants in the earlier cohorts also probably had less capital when they started their business in Hong Kong than those recent immigrants, because the former were more likely to be illegal immigrants from the poor and backward rural regions of Guangdong.

Recent immigrants, however, are legal immigrants who are more likely to have relatives in Hong Kong who can give them some financial support. They may also have taken advantage of the economic opportunities that arose after years of privatization and economic reform in the Mainland to accumulate some savings prior to immigration, whereas it was virtually impossible for immigrants in the earlier cohorts to accumulate savings in a centrally planned economy during the time of the Cultural Revolution. These two factors — capital and market exposure and information — could explain the differential performance (in terms of relative mean income with respect to native employers) of recent immigrant employers in the 1981 and 1996 cohorts.

The performance pattern of immigrants who are self-employed relative to natives is more complicated. The self-employed mean income gap between earlier immigrants and natives widened somewhat, from 4.2% in 1981 to 9.3% in 1996, but the gap between recent immigrants and natives narrowed considerably, from 14.3% to 2.5% over the same period. It is possible that the human capital of earlier immigrants acquired in the Mainland prior to immigration obsolesced in Hong Kong over time from 1981 to 1996 rather rapidly as the economy of Hong Kong restructured. In contrast, for reasons stated earlier, recent immigrants of 1996 are better informed and better prepared to participate in the Hong Kong economy prior to immigration than pre-1981 immigrants. This could explain the reverse pattern in the relative income of the self-employed for earlier and recent immigrants.

More research needs to be done to deepen our understanding of what determines the income of the self-employed and employers as opposed to the wage earnings of employees before we can be more definitive about the different patterns of relative income.

Notes

1. The first part of this chapter is substantially based on Lam and Liu (1997).

2. For details of the decomposition, see Lam and Liu (1997).

3. For details of the assumptions and the derivation of this result, see Lam and Liu (1997).

4. In Hong Kong, the percentage of youngsters in the relevant age cohort attending university in 1981 was about 3%. Most youngsters completed their schooling before the age of seventeen to nineteen. We have no information on the age distribution of the male immigrants of the pre-1981 arrival cohort at the time they arrived in Hong Kong. However, we have the age distribution of the 1976–81 arrival cohort from the 1981 Census, and it could be representative of the age distribution of earlier arrivals. About 67% of the new arrivals were aged twenty or above. Most of them would have ceased all schooling upon arrival in Hong Kong. Another revealing indicator is the mean age at which immigrants completed their schooling. The mean years of schooling of the pre-1981 arrival cohort are about seven years, implying that the mean age of immigrants when they completed their schooling is thirteen. More than 82% of the new arrivals in the 1976–81 arrival cohort were aged fourteen or above. Before the abolition of the reached-base policy, most illegal immigrants who crossed the border stealthily were adults who had completed their schooling in China.

5. See a report on continuing education of the University Grants Council (Chung, Ho, and Liu, 1994).

6. See Suen (1993). The index of sectoral shift in employment is defined as

$$I_t = \sum_j |e_{j,\,t} - e_{j,\,t-1}| / 2$$

where $e_{j,\,t}$ is the employment share of the jth industry in year t.

CHAPTER 8

Immigration and Earnings Inequality in Hong Kong

Immigration, Population Heterogeneity, and Inequality

In Chapter 7 we show that on average immigrants have lower earnings than Hong Kong natives. The arrival of immigrants swells the rank of low-income people. It has been argued that immigration increases earnings inequality in Hong Kong. In this chapter we show that increased immigration does not increase measured earnings inequality, but rather it *reduces* inequality. We base our argument on the statistical fact that when shares of population groups are shifted, the degree of inequality shifts too.

In this chapter, we first explain the meaning of population heterogeneity and its relation with a measure of income inequality. The next section is where more technical details of decomposing the earnings inequality are presented. How heterogeneity of Hong Kong's population contributes to inequality is then reported, followed by the empirical results of this chapter.[1]

Income inequality is usually represented by an aggregate summary measure such as the Gini ratio. A change in this ratio has always generated intense interest among economists as to the underlying causes. Heated debates among politicians and pressure groups often flare up as regards the possible income redistribution policy actions that should be taken to address the issue. In these debates, a change in the aggregate measure of inequality is often used as evidence to support or to argue against a certain income redistribution policy. However, the complexities of the statistical and economic processes that generate the change in the aggregate index are not well understood; often they are simply ignored.

To be more specific, if a population has heterogeneous groups that have different income-generating processes, a change in aggregate income inequality can be caused by a change in income dispersion within each population group, a change in population group structure, or a combination of both. Any policy, such as an immigration policy that changes the population structure could alter the aggregate inequality index substantially even though there may be little change in income dispersion within each population group. However, an immigration policy is often implemented with other policy objectives in mind, such as economic growth and family reunion rather than equity in income distribution. If population shift is an important factor leading to an increase in measured income inequality, a redistribution policy based on a change in the measured aggregate income inequality index without differentiating the sources of such change will be misguided.

In the section that follows this, we decompose an additively decomposable measure into within-group and between-group components. We show how shifts in shares of population groups could account for a substantial portion of the increase in measured income inequality. Specifically, we focus on the effect of the immigration policy on income inequality, since it is one of the few policies that could bring about a substantial shift in shares of population groups within a short time span to generate an observable impact on measured income inequality. We remove ("net out") the effect of population shifts, and then analyze the income dispersion within a population group in terms of a conventional human capital model.

Immigration has a heterogeneity effect and a wage effect on income inequality. By heterogeneity effect we mean the statistical effect on inequality as a result of the introduction of a group of immigrants whose income distribution is different from that of the indigenous population. Increase in heterogeneity affects inequality through shifts in shares of heterogeneous population groups that have different income dispersions. The heterogeneity effect has been the object of study in works on immigrants. For instance, Simon (1989) studied the dispersion of family income of immigrants as compared to natives. He found that the income dispersion of recent immigrants is less than that of natives. The finding implies that income distribution of the society as a whole becomes narrower as a result of immigration. Besides such an effect of income dispersion, there is also a wage effect of immigration.

The wage effect on income inequality arises from the differential impact of an inflow of immigrants on (1) wages and (2) unemployment (of natives and existing immigrants) in the indigenous labour market. In Chapter 6 we report that numerous studies show that the effects of immigration on native labour wage are insignificant. A similar study by Suen (1994) for Hong Kong yields the same result. Since the impact of immigration on wages seems negligible, the wage effect of immigration on income inequality is likely to be small and will not be considered further. We will rather concentrate on the heterogeneity effect.

During the fifteen years between the 1981 and 1996 censuses, there was a substantial shift in the composition of natives, immigrants, and other foreign workers in the population of Hong Kong. Total inequality (measured by variance of logarithmic earnings) increased by as much as 53.4% over the fifteen-year period. Rising inequality has aroused the attention of labour unions and community groups that exert pressure on the Hong Kong government to effect income redistribution to help the poor. It has also generated a debate among economists as to why inequality has increased so rapidly during a decade in which Hong Kong has experienced high growth. The inflow of immigrants, the importation of semi-skilled and unskilled foreign workers, the restructuring of the Hong Kong economy, and increasing monopolization have been put forward as possible causes of the rise in income inequality in the 1980s (see for instance Lin [1995], Suen [1994]).

Our analysis in this chapter shows that about one-quarter of the increase in measured inequality in Hong Kong is attributable to a change in the immigration policy that inadvertently increases measured inequality through shifts in population shares. Having isolated this effect, we conclude that the increase in inequality purely as a result of widening income dispersion is only about 60% of the measured increase in total inequality. This residual increase in inequality can be explained in the context of the conventional human capital model.

Decomposing Earnings Inequality into Within-Group and Between-Group Components

In decomposing the components that contribute to earnings inequality, we use the variance of logarithmic earnings as the primary measure of inequality. [2] The total inequality can be easily decomposed into a between-group and a within-group component, with the weights being the population share of groups.

Three concepts of inequality are therefore differentiated: The total inequality measuring the overall degree of inequality (for example the variance of logarithmic earnings), the between-group inequality measuring differences among various population groups (for example, between the natives and the immigrants), and within-group inequality reflecting the dispersion of income within each group.[3]

Changes in within- and between-group inequality over time can in turn be decomposed. For instance, a change in within-group inequality from 1981 to 1996 can be decomposed into a component caused by a change in variance of the population groups using 1981 group shares as weights, a component caused by a change in group shares, using 1981 log earnings variance as weights, and a component of interaction term. Such decomposition enables us to separate the effect on earnings inequality of a change in population group structure from that of a change in earnings dispersion itself. A formal model of decomposition appears in Appendix B.

We do not base our analysis on the Gini ratio, even though it is widely used in the study of income distribution. The main consideration is that even though the Gini ratio satisfies the three conditions of inequality measures, it is not additively decomposable. Neither do we not adopt the Theil L measure, even though it satisfies the three conditions and is additively decomposable; it is because the formula of the Theil measure is arbitrary and has little intuitive meaning.[4]

Heterogeneous Population Groups

Table 8.1 shows the shares and the characteristics of four population groups in the 1981 and 1996 censuses: natives, earlier Chinese immigrants, recent Chinese immigrants, and the group of "others" which consists of other foreign workers who were not born in the Mainland. These four population groups are heterogeneous in the sense that they have structurally different earnings generating processes.[5]

It is important to note that for reasons reported in Chapter 2, there was a significant decrease in the number of recent Chinese immigrants after October 1980 because of a change in the immigration policy. Consequently, the share of immigrants in the population fell. The large decline in the combined share of recent and earlier Chinese immigrants, from 0.4707 to 0.2829, is offset by the increase in the share of natives, from 0.5032 to 0.6110, and of the "others" group, from 0.0261 to 0.1061. This point is significant because in the next section we show the shift in population composition accounts for about one-quarter of the measured aggregate earnings inequality in Hong Kong from 1981 to 1996.

The group of "others" is made up of predominantly foreign workers from countries other than China who are admitted to Hong Kong on work visas. They usually work for a period without acquiring permanent residence. This is a heterogeneous group dominated by two large subgroups of workers: highly paid expatriate employees mainly from North America, Europe, and Australia and low-paid female domestic helpers mainly from the Philippines. The latter subgroup represents about one-third of the "others" group. Both are admitted into Hong Kong as long as they are sponsored by local employers, and there is no restriction by quota. The share of "others" more than tripled from 1981 to 1996.

Table 8.1
Characteristics of Earnings by Population Groups, 1981 and 1996

	Mean		Variance		Change in Variance during 1981–96	
	1981	1996	1981	1996	Amount	(%)
Natives						
Population share	0.5032	0.6110				
Median earnings	1,500	10,000				
Monthly earnings			1,853	13,988	2.49*	163*	160*	(6,448.0)
Log earnings			7.343	9.305	0.3195	0.4275	0.1080	**(33.8)**
Schooling			8.899	11.086	10.996	16.196	5.2004	(47.3)
Experience			12.838	16.090	97.792	117.513	19.7207	(20.2)
Earlier Immigrants						
Population share	0.3775	0.2539				
Median earnings	1,500	8,000				
Monthly earnings			1,823	10,313	2.31*	94.8*	92.4*	(3,998.4)
Log earnings			7.336	9.020	0.3196	0.3859	0.0663	**(20.8)**
Schooling			6.439	8.545	16.826	18.540	1.7142	(10.2)
Experience			30.464	28.063	196.869	184.171	−12.6980	(−6.5)
Recent Immigrants						
Population share	0.0932	0.0290				
Median earnings	1,200	7,500				
Monthly earnings			1,292	1,0391	0.374*	119*	118*	(31,638.0)
Log earnings			7.083	8.985	0.1631	0.4533	0.2902	(177.9)
Schooling			7.834	10.280	11.655	19.783	8.1285	(69.7)
Experience			14.843	17.844	108.722	131.743	23.0206	(21.2)
Others						
Population share	0.0261	0.1061				
Median earnings	1,500	5,500				
Monthly earnings						
Male			3,642	27,883	32.7*	777*	745*	(2,277.6)
Female			1,803	7,776	7.61*	137*	130*	(1,705.4)
All			3,034	14,534	25.2*	455*	429*	(1,703.7)
Log earnings						
Male			7.724	9.660	0.6876	0.9424	0.2548	(37.1)
Female			7.184	8.572	0.4589	0.4919	0.0330	(7.2)
All			7.545	8.983	0.6765	0.9406	0.2641	(39.0)
Schooling			9.985	12.349	17.709	22.253	4.5437	(25.7)
Experience			22.489	17.643	126.324	128.843	2.5191	(2.0)

Source: Table 7.4.

Note: * Variance figures are in millions (10^6). Interpretations of bold figures in the last column are made in the last section of this chapter.

The increase in the share of expatriates and foreign domestic workers at the two extremes of the earnings spectrum has had a significant effect on increasing earnings inequality in Hong Kong.

With regard to log earnings, Table 8.1 shows that the mean and variance of natives are higher than those of recent immigrants and earlier immigrants in 1981 and 1996. In particular, the mean earnings and the dispersion of earnings of recent immigrants are substantially lower than those of natives, indicating that recent immigrants are a more homogeneous low-earnings group.

In contrast, the "others" group has the highest mean earnings and earnings dispersion in the highest 1981 and 1996. The male subgroup is dominated by expatriate managerial and professional employees of high mean earnings; their incomes widen substantially over time. The female subgroup is dominated by foreign domestic helpers of low mean earnings. Their incomes have not widened much because the government has set a mandatory minimum wage for them. The increase in the number of female foreign domestic helpers has actually caused a decline in income spread of females in the "others" group. The income dispersion of the "others" group as a whole increases significantly by 0.2641 over the period, which is a much greater increase than the corresponding increase of 0.1080 for natives.

Empirical Results

Table 8.2 shows the overall earnings inequality as measured by the variance of log earnings, and its decomposition into within- and between-group inequality. It shows that total inequality increased substantially from 0.3212 in 1981 to 0.4944, or 53.4%. in 1996.[6] Decomposition shows that between-group inequality contributes only 2% to 5% to total inequality.

This implies that in any particular year, the presence of heterogeneous population groups *by itself* has only a minor effect on total inequality. Total inequality in any year is predominantly determined by within-group inequality, which accounts for over 95% of total measured inequality.

Table 8.2
Decomposition of Earnings Inequality, 1981 and 1996

	1981	1996
(1) Total measured inequality	0.3212 (100%)	0.4944 (100%)
(2) Within-group inequality	0.3143 (97.9%)	0.4724 (95.6%)
(3) Between-group inequality	0.0069 (2.5%)	0.0220 (4.4%)
(4) Total increase in inequality	0.1732 (100%)	
(5) Due to within-group increase	0.1581 (91.3%)	
(6) Due to between-group increase	0.0151 (8.7%)	

Table 8.3
Share of Population, Log Earnings Variance and Within-Group Inequality
by Population Groups, 1981 and 1996

1981 Population Group	Share of Population (a)	Log Earnings Variance (b)	Contribution to Within-Group Inequality (a) x (b)	
Natives	50.32%	0.3195	0.1608	(51.2%)
Earlier Chinese Immigrants	37.75%	0.3196	0.1206	(38.4%)
Recent Chinese Immigrants	9.32%	0.1631	0.0152	(4.8%)
Others	2.61%	0.6765	0.0177	(5.6%)
Total	100%		0.3143	(100%)

1996 Population Group	Share of Population (a)	Log Earnings Variance (b)	Contribution to Within-Group Inequality (a) x (b)	
Native	61.10%	0.4275	0.2612	(55.3%)
Earlier Chinese Immigrants	25.39%	0.3859	0.0980	(20.8%)
Recent Chinese Immigrants	2.90%	0.4631	0.0134	(2.8%)
Others	10.61%	0.9406	0.0998	(21.1%)
Total	100%		0.4724	(100%)

Source: Table 8.2, row 2 gives the figures 0.3143 and 0.4724 used in this Table.

With regard to the over time increase in total inequality, Table 8.2 shows that about 91% of the increase from 1981 to 1996 (0.1732) can be accounted for by an increase in within-group inequality (0.1581) with only the remaining 9% accounted for by an increase in between-group inequality (0.0151).

In what follows we ignore between-group inequality and focus on within-group inequality and its change. Within-group inequality is the result of variances of different population groups weighted by their population shares. Table 8.3 shows the contribution of each population group to within-group inequality. As expected, the main contribution comes from natives, because they are the largest population group. Their contribution to the inequality accounts for over half of the within-group inequality in any year.

It is instructive to decompose the change in within-group inequality from 1981 to 1996 into two components: one caused by a change in income dispersion and the other by a change in population share. The procedure of decomposition is detailed in Appendix B and the results are reported in Table 8.4. The amount of increase in within-group inequality between 1981 and 1986 was 0.4724 – 0.3143 = 0.1581. Using 1981 weights for decomposition, we can see that 24.4% of that increase is attributable to a change in population shares (column c). If 1996 weights are used, the contribution of the change in shares will be 27.8% (column f).

To summarize, the change in population shares accounts for about 24% to 28% of the increase in within-group inequality. This change is equivalent to about 22% to 25% of the increase in total inequality. We identify two main sources responsible for the increase: specifically, (1) the large reduction of the combined share of recent and earlier Chinese immigrants who have a relatively small earnings dispersion (rows 2 and 3 of Table 8.4, columns c and f); and (2) the corresponding increase in the share of natives and "others" who have a relatively large earnings dispersion (rows 1 and 4, columns c and f). Recent immigrants are by definition those who have been in the labour market for less than six years. They are relatively new entrants to the local labour market and their wage

Table 8.4
Decomposition of Change in Within-Group Inequality, 1981–96

Population Group	Change in Within-Group Inequality (1981–96) (a)	Decomposition with 1981 Weights			Decomposition with 1996 Weights		
		Change in Variance (b)	Change in Share (c)	Interaction Term (d)	Change in Variance (e)	Change in Share (f)	Interaction Term (g)
(1) Natives	0.1004	0.0544	0.0344	0.0116	0.0660	0.0461	−0.0116
(2) Earlier Immigrants	−0.0227	0.0250	−0.0395	−0.0082	0.0168	−0.0477	0.0082
(3) Recent Immigrants	−0.0018	0.0280	−0.0105	−0.0193	0.0087	−0.0297	0.0193
(4) Others	0.0821	0.0069	0.0541	0.0211	0.0280	0.0752	−0.0211
Total	0.1581	0.1143	0.0386	0.0053	0.1196	0.0439	−0.0053
	(100%)	(72.3%)	(24.4%)	(3.3%)	(75.6%)	(27.8%)	(−3.3%)

differentials are smaller than those of established workers, who are natives and expatriate workers.

Our analysis demonstrates that the inflow of recent Chinese immigrants *by itself* did not increase earnings inequality in any significant way. There are two reasons: (1) the wage effect through lowering native wages is negligible, and (2) the increase in between-group inequality that follows is also very small. On the contrary, the abolition of the reached-base policy in 1980 and the large reduction in the share of recent and earlier Chinese immigrants that followed did significantly increase the measured inequality because slowing the inflow of Chinese immigrants entailed the gaining in population share of natives and "others"; as a result natives and "others" have contributed a much larger log earnings variance to the total inequality.

The change in the immigration policy since 1980 has inadvertently increased total measured inequality significantly by changing the population shares of natives and "others" versus that of immigrants. This effect of the change in immigration policy on earnings inequality is one-off. If the immigration policy adopted after October 1980 continues to remain in effect with no major changes, then this effect would not show up when we compare measured earnings inequality between 1996 and the next census date.

In this connection, it should be noted that a change in the immigration policy could have other effects on the change in earnings inequality because, in general, different immigrant cohorts (for instance, legal versus illegal) admitted under different policy regimes may have different patterns of change in earnings dispersion over time as they stay longer in the receiving country. What is important in our present finding is that when there is a change in immigration policy as Hong Kong did in curtailing illegal immigration, it will bring about a substantial shift in the shares of heterogeneous population groups. This *by itself* could have a substantial effect on measured earnings inequality; such a compositional effect may mask other contributions to changes in equality. Economists and decision makers should be careful in interpreting data on changes in earnings inequality when there are significant shifts in population shares.

In comparison to that of Chinese immigrants, the increase in the inflow of other foreign workers is a significant factor contributing to the increase in inequality, since their population share increases substantially and their earnings variance is the largest (see Table 8.4, row 4). From the income redistribution policy point of view, one may argue that Hong Kong should be concerned about earnings inequality within the population of permanent residents and immigrants who are potential permanent residents. Foreign workers are sojourners who are transient members of Hong Kong society. Earnings inequality within that group and the increase the group introduces into the total measured inequality of Hong Kong should not be of the same policy concern or with the same priority as the rise in earnings inequality among the permanent residents and immigrants.

If changes attributed to shifts in population shares, to the "interaction term", and to the increase in variance of the "others" group are removed, then we obtain the net increase in within-group inequality of the remaining three population groups (natives, earlier immigrants and recent immigrants). It may be argued that society should mainly be concerned with such a "net" effect rather than the total effect. In that case, the rise in inequality net of other effects during 1981–96 was 0.1143 – 0.0069 = 0.1074, using 1981 weight. This is about 62% of the increase in the total measured inequality of 0.1732 from 1981 to 1996 (see Table 8.2, row 4). In other words, the magnitude of the increase in inequality not caused by the immigration policy or by the inflow of skilled expatriate workers and unskilled domestic helpers is found to be only about 60% of the measured increase. This residual of 60% is mainly a result of the increase in earnings dispersion within the three population groups increasing inequality. In the following section we will attempt to explain the changes that cause this increase in earnings dispersion within the population groups.

Human Capital Explanation of Inequality

It remains to be shown that the increases in the earnings dispersion of the three population groups of natives, earlier Chinese immigrants and recent Chinese immigrants over time is consistent with the human capital model.[7] The human capital model interprets schooling and experience as human capital investments that augment an individual's productivity. To the extent that earnings can be explained by such human capital variables, it follows that, *ceteris paribus*, the earnings dispersion of a population group depends on the variance in human capital investments (see Appendix C). Consequently, an increase in earnings dispersion over time will be driven by increasing variance in human capital investments. This is in general borne out by figures on the three population groups presented in Table 8.1. Specifically, the last column of Table 8.1 shows that increases in earnings inequality from 1981 to 1996 for natives (33.8%) and earlier Chinese immigrants (20.8%) are much smaller than the increase of 177.9% for recent immigrants (see Table 8.1). This is consistent with the smaller or negative to negligible increase in variance of schooling and experience for natives and earlier immigrants over the same period, and the large increase in variance of schooling (69.7%) and the sizeable increase in variance of experience (21.2%) for recent immigrants, in line with the prediction of the human capital model.

The 1981 cohort of recent Chinese immigrants is composed of mainly illegal immigrants with relatively homogeneous backgrounds who reached base in Hong Kong. They are predominantly young males with a low level of education and experience. The 1996 cohort of recent Chinese immigrants, on the other hand, is exclusively made up of legal immigrants with more diverse backgrounds; this observation is shown by the much larger variance in their schooling and experience. Through the earnings- generation process, these large increases in variance in human capital investments of the 1996 cohort over the 1981 cohort of immigrants translate into a sharp increase in earnings dispersion of this population group across the two censuses.

It should be noted that for all three population groups the percentage increase in the variance of log earnings (39%) is larger than the percentage increase in the variance of schooling (25.7%) and experience (2.0%). This indicates that while variance in human capital investments is a significant factor that explains earnings dispersion, it does not fully explain earnings inequality. There are other factors that contribute to the change in earnings inequality.

Notes

1. This chapter is substantially based on Lam and Liu (1998).

2. This measure has the desirable characteristics of being mean-independent, population-size independent, and satisfying the Pigou-Dalton condition that any transfer from a poorer person to a richer person should increase the inequality measure. See Sen (1973) for a discussion of the requirement of inequality indices. In the variance of log earnings measure, the Pigou-Dalton condition is not satisfied for incomes above ue where e is the base of the natural log and u is the geometric mean income of the distribution. For a more detailed discussion, see Anand (1983).

3. Within-group inequality comes about as a result of the aggregate contribution of log earnings variance within each heterogeneous group weighted by the respective population share. Between-group inequality is a result of the presence of heterogeneous groups that have mean log earnings different from the population mean. The variance of the difference in group mean is also weighted respectively by the population share to yield the between-group inequality.

4. Contributions obtained by decomposing the Theil measure are purely descriptive and do not follow known statistical distributions. In contrast, in the case of the log earnings variance measure, the ratio of within-group and between-group variance follows the F distribution, and statistical tests of significance can be performed when necessary. For a critique of the Theil L measure, see Sen (1973), p. 36.

5. Regressions of the Mincerian earnings functions of these population groups are structurally different. See Lam and Liu (1996).

6. The increase in the Gini ratio from 1981 to 1991 is from 0.382 to 0.427. See Suen (1993).

7. For a human capital theory of earnings inequality, see Becker (1964, 1967) and Mincer (1974). See also Liu and Wong (1981) for an application to Singapore data.

CHAPTER 9

Immigration Policy of Hong Kong: Assessment and Proposed Changes

The Prevailing Immigration Policy

The prevailing immigration policy that the Hong Kong Special Administrative Region (SAR) government inherits from the British is a passive one. The policy can no longer cope with the complexities of cross-border relations and with the integration between Hong Kong and South China. The objectives of the policy have been stated in numerous issues of the government's *Hong Kong Report*, the latest one of which came out in 1996. The objectives are described as follows: "Policies are framed to limit to an acceptable level population growth brought about by immigration, and to control the entry of foreign workers." (*Hong Kong Report*, 1997, p. 396)

The two objectives stated are both concerned with numbers. The way that they are phrased reflects the mindset of policy makers, who appear to believe that there are no other more worthy objectives — such as family reunion, humanitarian concerns, or the provision of skilled manpower for economic growth — than number control. Indeed, if the sole immigration policy objective is number control, the government should simply do its utmost to keep the flow of immigrants, legal or otherwise, to a minimum. In fact, since 1993 the Hong Kong government has been responding to pressure to speed up the admission of the long queue of Mainland spouses and children of Hong Kong residents; it has twice sought

131

an agreement with the Chinese authorities to increase the daily quota of immigration from the Mainland. It has also reacted to pressure from the business sector to admit Chinese citizens who have resided overseas, as well as professional and skilled personnel who now live in the Mainland, to work in Hong Kong. All of them could be granted permanent residence after a seven-year stay. Increasingly, the official objective of controlling numbers will come into conflict with the demands of the community.

A review of the history of immigration in Hong Kong in the last three decades shows that, even with regard to number control, there have been wild swings in policies (see Chapters 2 and 3). The immigration policy swung from a permissive to a restrictive one with regard to entry and residence in Hong Kong. This swing in policy and its implications have not been discussed and debated in the community in the context of the rapid developments in cross-border socio-economic integration in recent years.

The phrasing of the immigration policy objectives in terms of entry control is not merely semantic. It reflects the mindset of decision makers and it guides the actions of government officials who execute the policy in the Immigration Department. It explains why government officials insist on taking forcible action to separate babies and children from their mothers in the many heart-wrenching cases of repatriation. After all, family reunion and humanitarianism are not stated objectives in the immigration policy. Control of entry is.

One may argue that the former Hong Kong government should be absolved from blame for not pursuing a positive and proactive immigration policy with more worthwhile objectives than those of merely controlling entry. The government may be absolved on the grounds that it does not have the full authority to set its own policy. The Hong Kong government cannot determine the entry quota without the agreement of the Chinese authorities; nor can it receive and screen applications for immigration and determine who should be admitted (see Chapter 3). Constrained and with no sovereign authority, the Hong Kong government has had little leeway to pursue a more active immigration policy. Be that as it may, however, one should not be too quick to exonerate the government for failing to take early and decisive actions to tackle the problem of divided families across the border. Family reunion has never been the policy's guiding objective. This may explain why so little has been done to speed up the entry of Mainland spouses and children of Hong Kong residents into Hong Kong despite the long transition since the 1984 signing of the Joint Sino-British Declaration on the changeover of sovereignty. Only in 1993, a few years before 1 July 1997, did the Hong Kong government manage to increase the daily entry quota. It did so again in 1995, but the quota increase was too little too late.

The Hong Kong SAR government is now beset with the problems it inherited from the pre-1997 Hong Kong government because these problems had not been effectively resolved by the previous government. The prevailing immigration policy, therefore, must be changed.

What follows are ten proposals that we put forward to amend the present policy. In the main, they seek to support population growth (Proposal No. 1), clarify the objectives of the policy (No. 2), gain more control over the admission of immigrants (No. 3), promote family reunion (No. 4 to 7), limit welfare aid to new immigrants (No. 8), and increase the supply of skilled manpower to Hong Kong (No. 9 and 10).

An Immigration Policy to Support Population Growth

Proposal 1

Instead of limiting population growth, the new immigration policy should support it.

With a total fertility rate at 1.2 (children per couple), which is among the lowest in the world (see Table 5.2), the population of Hong Kong cannot replace itself in the long run through natural increase alone. Without the infusion of immigrants, the population

Table 9.1

Population Projections at Five-Year Intervals, 1996–2016

	Mid-1996 (base year)	Mid-2001	Mid-2006	Mid-2011	Mid-2016
Population					
(1) Aged 0–14	1,188,900	1,152,200	1,141,200	1,137,900	1,187,400
	(19)	(17)	(16)	(15)	(15)
(2) Aged 15–64	4,471,800	5,048,800	5,411,200	5,768,400	5,926,800
	(71)	(72)	(73)	(74)	(72)
(3) Aged 65 and over	631,300	750,000	830,200	890,800	1,091,700
	(10)	(11)	(11)	(11)	(13)
Total	6,292,000	6,951,000	7,382,600	7,797,100	8,205,900
	(100)	(100)	(100)	(100)	(100)
Annual Growth Rate (over a five-year period)	2.0%	1.2%	1.1%	1.0%	
Dependency Ratio					
(4) Child Dependency Ratio	266	228	211	197	200
(5) Elderly Dependency Ratio	141	149	153	155	184
(6) Overall Dependency Ratio	407	377	364	351	384
Median age	34	37	39	40	41

Source: Census and Statistics Department's projections based on the 1996 by-census.

Note: Percentage of population in parentheses.
Row(4) = Row(1) / Row(2); Row(5) = Row(3) / Row(2); Row(6) = Row(4) + Row(5), with a unit of "per 1,000 population aged 15–64."

will theoretically shrink toward zero (see Chapter 5). Long before that happens, the shrinking of the labour force will result in severe labour shortage, production bottlenecks and economic stagnation. The population as a whole will age, and the dependency ratio will increase. Supporting the elderly will become increasingly burdensome for the working population, and the standard of living will decline.

The early 1980s was a watershed period for the society of Hong Kong. The reached-base policy was abandoned, and the total fertility rate fell below 2.0. Since that period, the flow of legal immigrants has been the major demographic factor to keep the population of Hong Kong growing (see Chapter 5). Given the important contribution of immigration to population growth, the immigration policy should be framed with a positive objective of supporting population growth rather than with the negative one at present.

The population growth rate has fluctuated over the last several decades, mainly on account of the continual influx of illegal immigrants, and of the flow of return migrants, especially in the last few years. In the medium term, an annual population growth rate of 2% appears to be an appropriate target. This assessment is based on the historical experience of Hong Kong's labour market. Population growth rates of close to 3% or higher have been recorded in the periods 1973–74 and 1979–81. These periods were characterized by negative growth in real wages and a relatively high unemployment rate of over 3%. Such developments appeared during those two periods and in the years that immediately followed. On the other hand, following periods of population growth rate of less than 2%, as in the periods 1975–78 and 1982–92, real wages tended to increase markedly, and the unemployment rate fell to below 2% (see Tables 5.5, 5.9, and 5.11). To maintain a moderate rate of increase in real wages with a low unemployment rate, and to sustain economic growth with a steady supply of labour with no production bottlenecks caused by labour shortage, a population growth rate target of around 2% seems desirable. The question is whether there is further room to increase admissions of legal immigrants within this target rate.

Based on the 1996 By-Census, the Census and Statistics Department projects for the period 1997–2016 that the population of Hong Kong will increase at an average annual growth rate of 1.3%, from 6.29 million in mid-1996 to 7.38 million in mid-2006 and to 8.21 million in mid-2016. The population will age considerably. Its median age will rise from thirty-four in 1996 to forty-one in 2016. It is projected that the proportion of the population aged sixty-five or above will increase from 10% in 1996 to 13% in 2016 (see Table 9.1). This projection is based on the assumption that the daily quota for one-way permits for legal immigrants from the Mainland is maintained at 150, yielding a total of 1.1 million Chinese immigrants for the twenty-year period 1997–2016 who will make up 57% of the population growth for the period. Natural increase (i.e. births less deaths) and net movements of Hong Kong residents and persons holding foreign travel documents (including expatriates and foreign domestic helpers) account for the remaining 25% and 18%, respectively.

Table 9.1 shows that the projected population growth rate for the first five years of the twenty-year period is 2%, which falls to between 1% and 1.2% for the rest of the period, mainly on the assumption that the net movement of Hong Kong residents who hold Hong Kong permanent identity cards or travel documents — increased rapidly since 1993 — will slow down in 1998 and turn negative again in 1999 and afterward. The case in favour of Proposal 1 is therefore stated in brief as follows: With an average projected annual population growth rate at only 1.3% (from 1997 to 2016), and a profile of growth rates to fall from 2% in 2001 to 1% in 2016, there is plenty of room to promote population growth. We propose that this growth be achieved by increasing the daily quota of one-way permits to meet the growth rate target of 2% per annum, unless the government's growth projection is grossly underestimated.

Clear Enunciation of the Objectives of the Immigration Policy

Proposal 2

The objectives of a new immigration policy should be set after consultation and debate and it should then be clearly enunciated to the public.

The immigration policy affects the future of Hong Kong and the lives of many people, especially those who have family members still residing in the Mainland. It is significant that the public has never been consulted on such an important policy, whereas wide consultation on issues of much less impact, such as trade effluent charging or a common carrier system for the gas supply, has been conducted. Perhaps this has been because, unlike that of a sovereign country, the former Hong Kong government did not have control of the number of immigrants and individuals it could admit. The Hong Kong SAR government should now break this mode of policy drift and seize the initiative.

There are inherently conflicting interests involved in setting immigration policy objectives. If we emphasize the economic role of immigration and if we advocate admitting more professional and skilled personnel, it could be at the expense of the objective of reuniting families. If we facilitate family reunion, we may deprive Hong Kong of much-needed skilled manpower. An immigration policy has to balance political, economic, social, humanitarian, and philosophical considerations, and the way to achieve this balance is through public consultation and debate. There is always a risk of dividing the community in any policy debate, especially one as sensitive as immigration. However, the risk of not setting an immigration policy or of setting one without public support is even greater. In a policy vacuum, people could react to policies or ad hoc measures that they do not understand or support by directing their hostility towards immigrant groups in the population. At the end, hostility and prejudice growing out of misunderstanding and ignorance could be socially more divisive than an informed, open debate on the policy.

Greater Control of Admissions

Proposal 3

The Hong Kong SAR government must exercise control over who should be admitted into Hong Kong as immigrants.

To have a meaningful immigration policy that it can implement effectively, the Hong Kong SAR government must have authority in deciding who should be admitted as immigrants. Under British rule it had not been possible for Hong Kong to control immigration from the Mainland, because China did not recognize the three unequal treaties that ceded Hong Kong and leased the New Territories to Britain. China has always insisted that Chinese citizens should have freedom of movement in and out of Hong Kong (see Chapter 2). The Hong Kong government has in the past agreed with China on the daily quota of legal immigrants holding one-way permits issued by Chinese authorities that could enter Hong Kong without screening each individual case. All immigrants from the Mainland holding one-way permits issued within the quota have been automatically accepted. This situation continues to this date (in early 1998).

When Hong Kong was under British rule, there was no possibility that China would concede that "British Hong Kong" had the right to screen and approve applications for immigration from China. Since 1 July 1997 sovereignty is no longer an issue. There is no reason why the Chinese government should insist on the freedom of movement of Chinese citizens into Hong Kong. In fact under the "one country, two systems" framework, the border between Hong Kong SAR and Shenzhen remains, and entry into Hong Kong is restricted.

Article 22 of the Basic Law is explicit about the authority and the limits of the Chinese government with regard to Chinese citizens entering Hong Kong. It states that: "For entry into the Hong Kong Special Administrative Region, people from other parts of China must apply for approval. Among them, the number of persons who enter the Region for the purpose of settlement shall be determined by the competent authorities of the Central People's Government after consulting the government of the Region."

The Article clearly specifies that the Central People's Government can determine the number of immigrants in consultation with the Hong Kong SAR government. It also states, without specifying who has the approving authority, that people from other parts of China who want to enter Hong Kong must apply for approval. According to logic and common practice, it should be the government of the region or country that immigrants intend to enter rather than the government of the region or country of origin that should approve entry applications. Throughout the world, individuals enjoy the freedom to leave a country (with a few notable exceptions), but the freedom to enter another country is without exception always restricted and subject to the approval of the receiving country. For a sovereign country, the approving authority is clear. Even for regions within a country, there are precedents in the Mainland that vest the authority for approving entrants with the receiving region. For instance, for entry across the second line into the Shenzhen SEZ, people from other parts of China must apply for permits that are approved by authorities of the Shenzhen SEZ. Even though the management of the second line of the Shenzhen SEZ has not been very tight, and entry authorization has not been always strictly enforced, it does not detract from the principle that the *receiving* region should decide who can enter. Since the regions concerned are all within China, national sovereignty is not an issue with regard to inter-regional mobility of people. Only the inter-regional relationship would be a concern.

The control of immigration with regard to number and composition is so vital to the future development of Hong Kong that the SAR government must negotiate with Beijing to recover the authority for approving applications for immigration from the Mainland under Article 22 of the Basic Law. The government can concede that the number should be decided on the basis of mutual agreement. As Chapter 3 clearly states, different local Chinese government bureaus exercise authority in deciding who can immigrate to Hong Kong. That has been the cause of long queue of spouses and children waiting for family reunion, and the source of complaint about inequity and injustice in the approval process. By taking control, the Hong Kong SAR government can replace the present system with an approval process that is more equitable, transparent, and accountable to the public.

To take over the task of receiving and approving applications for immigration may entail setting up immigration offices in key locations in the Mainland. Setting them up would be costly, but it is so important that the Hong Kong SAR government should not avoid it just because of the costs involved. Local Chinese authorities could be solicited to help collect applications and verify the authenticity of relevant documents on behalf of the Hong Kong SAR government, but it should be made clear to the applicants that only the Hong Kong SAR government has the authority to approve their applications.

Family Reunion: The Primary Objective

Proposal 4

The Hong Kong SAR government should identify family reunion as the primary objective of its immigration policy.

After gaining control over who should be admitted into Hong Kong as immigrants, the Hong Kong SAR government should identify the objectives of its immigration policy after public consultation. We propose that there should be two major objectives: family reunion and the supply of skilled manpower for the economy. The primary objective, however, should be family reunion. In other countries, immigration policies may have subsidiary objectives, including, for instance, providing an asylum for refugees and attracting prospective investors to invest in the country. However, in the context of Hong Kong, there appears to be no public support for turning the territory into a place that offers asylum for refugees. Also, as Hong Kong is not short of capital, there is no need to make special provision with regard to immigration to attract investments.

The arguments for identifying family reunion as the primary objective of an immigration policy are compelling. Among advanced economies whose living standards are comparable to those of Hong Kong, Hong Kong is perhaps one of the strictest on the subject of family reunion. The waiting period for legal immigrants (over 90% of whom are spouses or children of Hong Kong residents) before being admitted into Hong Kong is rather long. Table 3.5 shows half of them waited over two years, while 10% had to wait over five years with some having to wait as long as ten to twenty years. The waiting period for immediate family members is unacceptably long by the standard of advanced countries. In advanced countries, immediate family members of citizens are invariably given top priority and are granted permission to enter as immigrants for family reunion within a matter of months.

Behind the statistics of Table 3.5 are many tragic cases of families divided and separated for years by a border and an immigration policy callously conceived and enforced. Nothing speaks louder than the images of mothers and children, crying in despair, torn from one another and herded into vans to be repatriated across the border. What makes it even more heart-wrenching is that most of those forcibly separated and repatriated have husbands or fathers who are legal residents of Hong Kong. For months before 1 July 1997 television programmes abounded with scenes of families united and then broken apart. These images of inhumane treatment of spouses and children of our fellow residents will stay in the memories of many Hong Kong people. The human costs of such a policy are immense.

Even though the divided families bear the human cost of separation, society will not be spared the social costs. The current policy that divides families results in a large number of single-parent families on both sides of the border. Many youngsters who eventually will enter Hong Kong and become residents grow up in isolation and separated from their fathers or mothers. They are frustrated and humiliated, afraid and distressed. Unless they are guided in a proper direction, they will grow up feeling alienated from society, which they perceive as having mistreated their families. Hong Kong will ultimately pay the price when a significant number of the tens of thousands of these youths grow up to be delinquents and misfits in a society which does not welcome them in the first place. No amount of public spending on counselling and social welfare will be able to rectify some of the social problems we are creating for ourselves (Wong, 1997a).

The social costs of divided families are objective economic and social arguments for an immigration policy that promotes family reunion. The humanitarian arguments are just as compelling. A society, particularly a society of immigrants like Hong Kong's, should be compassionate toward those members of the community whose families are divided by a border. Almost every ethnic Chinese in Hong Kong is an immigrant or has an immigrant origin. Illegal immigrants of earlier cohorts who arrived in Hong Kong before the abolition of the reached-base policy were more fortunate, because there were then different ways, including illegal entry, by which to bring their family members to Hong Kong to settle. Given their immigrant root, Hong Kong people should be sympathetic to the plight of those less fortunate legal residents who still have immediate family members living across the border. But in fact antipathy and even hostility have been the rather common reactions of a considerable number of Hong Kong people, many of whom being former immigrants, toward these divided families when repatriation of mothers and children who entered illegally became a hot issue in the months before the changeover of sovereignty. The response of these former immigrants towards potential immigrants is no doubt motivated by selfishness. They fear that new immigrants will take away their jobs and that new immigrants not seeking jobs will live on public assistance at the expense of the community. Organized labour is at least indirectly responsible for fanning the flames of these fears.

To identify family reunion as the primary policy objective of immigration, the Hong Kong SAR government must seek broad-based community support for its policy. This is achieveable if the policy is made transparent and the public is consulted so that issues like the positive contribution of immigration to an otherwise shrinking population (see Chapter 5), the negligible impact of immigration on wages (see Chapter 6), the minor effect on increased earnings inequality (see Chapter 8), the eligibility of immigrants for welfare (see Chapter 6), and the immigrant roots of our community (see Chapter 2) can be thoroughly discussed and debated. The public will come to see that immigration is not only beneficial but is also indispensable to the viability and vitality of our population, and that if we accept immigration, then reunion of immediate family members of legal residents must be given high priority.

A Non-Discriminatory Policy on Family Reunion

Proposal 5

The policy on family reunion should be non-discriminatory with regard to country of origin.

The current policy of restricting entry of immigrants from the Mainland for family reunion under a quota is discriminatory. If a Hong Kong permanent resident marries a woman and has children in the Mainland, his family members will be subject to a long wait, sometimes as long as ten to twenty years (see Table 3.5), before being admitted to Hong Kong for family reunion. However, if a Hong Kong permanent resident marries a woman in any country outside China, treatment will be entirely different. He can at any time bring his wife and his children born in that country to Hong Kong on visitor visas. After entry, they can immediately apply for residence visas. The children only require a validation on their foreign passports to confirm that they are eligible for permanent residence in Hong Kong, and that can be done immediately after entry. As for the wife, if she is not herself already a permanent resident, she can apply for an extension of her visa at regular intervals until she becomes a permanent resident after seven years of residence. All procedures can be handled either before or after the entire family enters Hong Kong. The family is never separated, nor do immediate family members endure a long wait before they can enter Hong Kong.

The treatment of immediate family members (in the Mainland) of Hong Kong permanent residents is so discriminatory that they are even worse off than are family members of expatriates who come to work in Hong Kong on employment visas. Expatriate professionals and managers are allowed to bring their families with them without having to worry about quotas.

Table 9.2
Legal Immigration to Hong Kong by Status of Admission, 1983–95

Status of Admission	1983	1984	1985	1986	1987	1988	1989	1990	1991	1992	1993	1994	1995
Legal Entrants for Residence (from China)	26,701	27,475	27,285	27,111	27,268	28,137	27,263	27,976	26,782	28,367	32,909	38,218	45,986
With Employment Visas													
Technicians	846	986	1,224	1,042	1,276	1,261	1,709	2,348	2,223	2,610	2,547	2,211	1,934
Construction workers	187	46	10	45	15	94	125	7	43	11	32	n.a.	n.a.
Restaurant workers	100	98	136	114	130	190	209	468	463	422	409	n.a.	n.a.
Domestic workers	7,456	6,499	8,454	8,845	11,792	14,735	18,870	22,145	26,083	28,091	32,093	34,053	26,766
Other professionals and middle managers	1,747	2,024	2,612	2,893	3,281	3,895	4,569	4,765	4,679	4,932	6,555	7,547	6,130
Other*	2,235	2,148	2,049	2,322	2,589	3,260	3,242	3,237	3,699	4,358	6,158	7,355	5,695
Subtotal	12,571	11,801	14,485	15,261	19,083	23,435	28,724	32,970	37,190	40,424	47,794	51,166	40,525
With Residence Visas													
To join husband	3,064	3,229	3,654	3,587	4,447	5,376	4,733	5,072	5,920	6,919	7,335	7,627	6,739
To join wife	146	141	140	126	541	577	472	558	740	651	713	805	1,183
To join parents	2,805	3,076	3,593	3,663	4,698	5,669	5,772	5,146	5,025	5,595	6,292	6,126	5,162
To join son or daughter	646	593	821	925	777	775	716	781	787	811	832	917	963
Former resident	624	494	504	320	302	136	90	96	59	87	36	26	30
Right to land	2,740	3,351	4,709	5,195	7,057	7,795	8,197	8,657	10,088	12,505	14,529	14,404	13,865
To join relatives, widows or widowers	11	17	20	29	18	22	14	7	15	8	6	3	1
To join relatives	97	65	97	61	29	21	41	32	30	25	31	1	17
Miscellaneous	78	130	188	172	136	91	29	40	33	17	6	4	17
Others	9	2	6	7	2	10	12	0	8	16	17	5	34
Subtotal	10,220	11,098	13,732	14,085	18,007	20,472	20,076	20,389	22,705	26,634	29,797	29,918	28,011
Total	49,492	50,374	55,502	56,459	64,358	72,044	76,063	81,335	86,677	95,425	110,500	119,302	114,522

Sources: Immigration Department, Hong Kong Government.

Note: The above statistics do not include: (a) British citizens or United Kingdom belongers; (b) dependents from Vietnam, Laos and Cambodia; (c) persons from China via Macau unless the application was settled in Macau by 14 January 1979. n.a. means not available.

*Includes representatives of overseas companies and salesmen, trainees, sportsmen and entertainers.

Table 9.2 shows the different categories of legal immigrants from 1983 to 1995. In 1995 alone 7,922 immigrants entered Hong Kong from countries other than China to join their spouses, 5,162 to join their parents, and 963 to join their sons and daughters, and all were granted residence visas. These 14,047 entrants were not subject to any quotas or long waits before they could enter Hong Kong for the purpose of family reunion. To put the discriminatory treatment in perspective, this group should be compared to the group of 45,986 legal immigrants from the Mainland admitted under quotas in 1995 (94.1% were for family reunion as shown in Table 3.6) whose waiting period ranged from less than one year to over twenty-five years (see Table 3.5). The discrimination against marrying and having children in the Mainland as well as against people in the Mainland is striking. It is hard to believe that this grossly discriminatory practice can be tolerated in Hong Kong after reunification with China and at a time when there is so much social concern surrounding much finer aspects of equal opportunity, gender discrimination, and discrimination against the disabled.

When the Hong Kong SAR government recovers control over the approval of immigration applications from the Mainland, as is suggested in Proposal 3, it will be possible to eliminate this discrimination which is politically sensitive and morally repugnant. This can be achieved by either one of two ways: First, facilitate entry from the Mainland for family reunion to the same extent as for those entering from other countries. Second, delay entry from other countries for family reunion by imposing quotas like the ones imposed on those wishing to immigrate from the Mainland. As we will argue below, the first approach is preferred.

Immediate Entry of Children with Right-of-Abode and their Mothers (Fathers)

Proposal 6

The Hong Kong SAR government should announce that Mainland-born children of Hong Kong permanent residents who are entitled to the right of abode in Hong Kong under the Basic Law can enter Hong Kong with their mothers (or fathers) for family reunion at any time they choose and that their entry is not restricted by quota.

The Hong Kong SAR government estimates that there are about 66,000 such children. After years of warning, the Hong Kong government did not put into practice effective and timely measures before the changeover of sovereignty to facilitate and to prepare for their entry. Faced with an imminent crisis, only a few days after the changeover, the Hong Kong SAR government rushed an Immigration Amendment Bill through the Provisional Legislative Council on 10 July 1997 to require these children to apply in the Mainland for a certificate of entitlement for the right of abode and to stay there for approval before coming to Hong Kong (see Chapter 3). The government's legal position was that leaving the Mainland to enter Hong Kong without prior approval violates the laws of the Mainland and that its action is within the provision of the Basic Law. The government claimed that it could arrange for all eligible children to be admitted into Hong Kong within two years.

The Hong Kong SAR government's hastily passed legislation was challenged in the court by counsel representing a number of children who were smuggled into Hong Kong and who surfaced after 1 July 1997 to demand their right of abode. The argument against the government's position is that these children's right of abode is guaranteed by the Basic Law. This is a constitutional right that automatically became effective on 1 July 1997. The SAR government cannot use administrative measures to infringe on or circumscribe this right. Nor can it delay the children's exercising of their right. The fact that the children violated Mainland laws by leaving the Mainland without permission is not relevant to their right of abode in Hong Kong under the "one country, two systems" framework. The legal battle will be settled perhaps ultimately by the Court of Final Appeal.

Legal arguments aside, there are sound economic, social, and humanitarian reasons for admitting Mainland-born children who can prove that they are eligible for the right of abode as soon as possible. We have discussed the social and human costs of divided families across the border. The economic argument is also cogent. If these children ultimately are to be admitted into Hong Kong, it is better to bring them early to educate them rather than bringing them later. The rate of return to schooling investments of immigrants in the Mainland is not only much lower, but it also falls farther behind the rate of return to schooling acquired in Hong Kong (see Chapter 7). Educating these immigrant children in Hong Kong when they are young will help them to integrate better into the society and the economy of Hong Kong. It will bring higher economic returns both to the individuals and to society than educating them late when they come to Hong Kong as teenagers.

It is proposed that the Hong Kong SAR government should make a public announcement that any child who is entitled to the right of abode will be admitted at any time that his/her sponsoring parents present identification documents that can prove his/her entitlement to the satisfaction of the SAR government. The child should be admitted together with immediate family members. The SAR government should make transparent the type of documents that applicants should file to support their cases. Since admission would not be subject to quota and could be effected at any time, the entry of every potential applicants whose right of abode is genuine would be assured. They would have the incentive to complete the documentation of their identity and the application process in the Mainland instead of trying to enter Hong Kong through smuggling.

To further deter the smuggling of potentially eligible children into Hong Kong to stay while applications are being filed, the SAR government can do a preliminary screening of the eligibility of the children who file their applications in Hong Kong. Those who can provide *prima facie* evidence of eligibility will be allowed to stay temporarily to complete the documentation, while those who fail the screening will be repatriated immediately. Since the eligibility of those children who are allowed to stay temporarily has yet to be established, their accompanying family members (including their mothers) who are not Hong Kong residents will be repatriated as illegal immigrants. Also, if eligibility is eventually rejected and the right of abode is denied, the children will be repatriated, and the sponsoring parents will be levied a substantial fine for harbouring illegal immigrants, which could be made proportional to the length of stay of the children in Hong Kong.

To implement this policy, it would be necessary to request that the Chinese government agree to admissions that are outside the agreed-upon quota.[1] Mainland-born children with the right of abode and their immediate family members should be admitted with no restriction as to their number, while other immigrants should continue to be admitted under an agreed-upon quota.

The implementation of the proposed policy would be easier if the Hong Kong SAR government gains control over who can be admitted into Hong Kong, because Hong Kong can then receive applications directly from parents of these Mainland-born children. Otherwise, under the current arrangement, it will have to rely on the Chinese authorities to receive applications, to collect documents for verification by the SAR government, and to inform successful applicants. To continue doing this will reduce the credibility of the commitment of the Hong Kong SAR government to the new policy of unlimited admission of children with the right of abode and their immediate family members.

The proposed policy has numerous advantages over the policy adopted by the Hong Kong SAR government on 10 July 1997. The crux of the new policy is the assurance of admission at any time the successful applicants wish, and that makes all the difference. With this assurance and with the erection of other punitive measures against smuggling, parents of eligible children would probably not risk the lives of their children by smuggling them into Hong Kong in order to file applications there. Parents would then file applications for their children in the Mainland, and in fact, even when approval is given, they may not necessarily bring their children to Hong Kong immediately since they are assured that they will be welcome at any time. They would instead make the proper living arrangements and find the optimal time to bring their children to Hong Kong. This helps to space out the arrivals of these children somewhat and to avert the rush into Hong Kong.

The new policy will practically eliminate the smuggling of eligible children into Hong Kong because it will provide assurance, whereas the one adopted by the SAR government does not do so because of the uncertainty concerning the length of the waiting period. Parents of Mainland-born children may not find credible the government's present estimation that all eligible children could be processed and admitted within two years, especially considering that the number of eligible children is perceived to be underestimated. Under the policy passed by the Provisional Legislative Council, since admission continues to be constrained by a strict quota, and since the estimation of the number of eligible children is not credible, there is much uncertainty concerning the period of waiting. Parents will still arrange to have children smuggled into Hong Kong while applications are being processed and will smuggle them out of Hong Kong back to the Mainland when they are required to present themselves.

Given that neither policy will eliminate the smuggling of ineligible children, however, if the new policy is supplemented with a policy of giving priority to reunion of immediate family members under the quota system as we will discuss shortly under Proposal 7, the pressure to smuggle into Hong Kong children who are not eligible for the right of abode will ease considerably.

By guaranteeing that any children assessed as eligible for the right of abode can enter Hong Kong at any time, the new policy honours Hong Kong's commitment to these children as expeditiously as possible. It is consistent with both the letter and the spirit of Article 24 of the Basic Law. It gives the choice to the parents of when they will arrange for their Mainland-born children to come to Hong Kong and promotes family reunion and family values. Last but not least, it enables the orderly entry of eligible children, albeit perhaps at a slightly quicker pace than the policy adopted by the Hong Kong SAR government in July 1997.

The policy adopted by the SAR government now does seem to ensure orderly entry spread out over a period of about two years (if this time estimation is actually realized), but all the present policy achieves over and above our proposed one is that it gives the SAR government one to two more years to prepare for the provision of public services, such as schooling and social services, to receive this large number of immigrant children. This extra time, however, is gained at the expense of violating the right of these children and the Basic Law at least in spirit if not also in letter, and further frustrating their families. If an extra one or two years of delay in the entry of these children were essential, the government should have planned ahead to make schools and social services available far before 1 July 1997.

The proposed policy would enable a large number of eligible children, perhaps a large fraction of the estimated 66,000, to arrive in Hong Kong within a short span of time. Can Hong Kong cope with this sudden surge of immigrant children and their mothers? Hong Kong has plenty of experience in receiving and integrating large influxes of immigrants over its history (see Chapter 2). The last influx entered between 1978 and 1980, when over 300,000 illegal Chinese immigrants crossed the border into Hong Kong. Hong Kong was able to absorb large influxes of illegal immigrants in the past, when the community was much less affluent. There is no reason to believe that an affluent society like Hong Kong's in 1997 cannot do it again. Surely there will be dislocation and congestion in certain public services and facilities, but the problem should be temporary and not insurmountable.

Children who are admitted into Hong Kong for family reunion will most likely stay with their parents. Their accommodation is mainly a private problem of crowding within their family units. There could be a spillover effect on the provision of public housing due to greater demand for larger public rental units, but this would be a long-term effect. The abrupt increase in the number of immi-grant children will add pressure to the public health and transportation systems, causing some congestion, but the marginal increase in demand for services should not be too large. The most serious problem is that of the provision of primary and secondary school places for these children. The government is planning to build 16 more schools to accommodate the increase, but this will take time. The immediate solution is to temporarily reverse the policy of reducing primary school class size from forty-two to thirty-five, to delay the conversion of half-day sessions to full-day sessions in primary schools, and, if necessary, to re-introduce floating classes in schools located in districts of high immigrant concentration. These measures obviously will roll back some of the advances in improving educational quality, but the setback will only be temporary. The community as a whole will pay the price of delayed improvement in educational quality because the government has not planned adequately for the arrival of this large number of immigrant children despite years of warning of its eventuality.

Fine-Tuning Quotas to Facilitate Family Reunion

Proposal 7

Quotas should be fine-tuned to enable immediate family members of Hong Kong residents who do not have the right of abode to be reunited with minimal delay.

In line with the primary objective of family reunion (Proposal 4) and the policy of non-discrimination (Proposal 5), immediate family members (i.e. spouses and children) of Hong Kong residents who are ineligible for the right of abode under Article 24 of the Basic Law should be allowed to come to Hong Kong as soon as possible for family reunion. Under Proposal 6, Mainland-born children who have the right of abode and their immediate family members will be given unlimited entry outside the quota. The Hong Kong SAR government can probably reduce the daily quota and still accommodate other immigrants for family reunion. Top priority should be given to immediate family members of Hong Kong residents. The daily quota can be fine-tuned to enable them to be admitted with essentially no delay once their applications are approved. To discourage illegal entry and smuggling across the border, applicants for immigration with no right of abode should be required to submit their applications in the Mainland and to stay there until approved.

The unlimited entry of Mainland-born children with the right of abode will be initially very large as the backlog of eligible children is being cleared but will soon fall to a stable flow. Consisting of within- and outside-quota admissions, the total intake can be fine-tuned to attain the target population growth of 2% per annum over the medium term.

Under this proposal, spouses of Hong Kong residents living in the Mainland will effectively be able to enter Hong Kong as soon as they get married, in the same way that spouses of Hong Kong residents living in other countries can. Eliminating the waiting period of Mainland spouses — in most cases wives — of Hong Kong residents could change the quality and quantity of cross-border marriages. Hitherto, Mainland women marry Hong Kong men (or vice versa) with the expectation that it will take years before they and their children can immigrate to Hong Kong to be reunited with their husbands (or wives). This constraint limits the number of Mainland women (or men) who are willing to enter into cross-border marriages to perhaps those who have less choices of marriage partners, namely those who are less educated and who have limited or no economic opportunities. By changing the policy, the choice set of Hong Kong people who take Mainland spouses will be widened to include those who are better educated with higher skills and better economic prospects in the labour market, because cross-border marriage will become more attractive (Wong, 1997c). Hence, it is quite possible that the level of human capital endowment of Mainland spouses of Hong Kong residents will increase under the new policy. These better-educated spouses could add to the skilled labour force after immigration to Hong Kong and could also enhance the human capital investment of their offspring. This can only be beneficial to Hong Kong.

Whether the new policy will increase the frequency of Hong Kong males marrying Mainland females is an open and difficult question. More research needs to be done on why Hong Kong men marry Mainland women under the current restrictive policy. It is possible that many of those who marry across the border belong to the cohorts of young, less-educated illegal immigrants who rushed into Hong Kong in the 1978–80 wave, which precipitated the abolition of the reached-base policy. The arrival of the large number of young male illegal immigrants severely skewed the gender ratio of Hong Kong in the early 1980s (see Table 4.2). Mostly unskilled and earning low incomes, these men might have difficulty finding local Hong Kong brides even after they are established in Hong Kong. After gaining permanent residence in Hong Kong, many of them eventually return to their home villages in Guangdong to marry Mainland women. If that is the case, the number of cross-border marriages will fall after the 1978–80 wave of young illegal immigrants are past the normal marriage age. The number of cross-border marriages may settle down to a lower level despite the fact that they will have become more attractive to both parties under the new policy. In any case, once the current backlog of spouses and children waiting to be reunited with their families in Hong Kong is cleared under the new policy, the number will decrease.

Tightening the Eligibility of New Immigrants for Public Assistance

Proposal 8

The residence requirement of new immigrants for the Comprehensive Social Security Assistance (CSSA) should be lengthened from one year to two.

Under Proposals 6 and 7, it would be much easier for dependents of Hong Kong residents to immigrate to Hong Kong. Welfare dependence could increase as a result. To discourage recent immigrants to depend on public assistance, and to encourage the sponsoring Hong Kong residents to make financial plans to provide for their spouses and Mainland-born children before bringing them to Hong Kong, it is proposed that the residence requirement for CSSA be lengthened from one year to two.

Lengthening the residence requirement for CSSA should not cause immigrants who come to Hong Kong for family reunion undue hardship, as they should be taken care of by their family members in Hong Kong when they come. Lengthening the requirement will oblige their family members in Hong Kong to make adequate financial provisions before sponsoring their relatives' immigration. The relaxation of immigration restrictions for family reunion purposes coupled with a tightening of public assistance eligibility will reduce the social costs of family separation and make the immigration policy more humane without burdening society with increased welfare costs.

Supply of Skilled Manpower: The Secondary Objective

Proposal 9

The Hong Kong SAR government should identify the supply of skilled manpower for the economy as the secondary objective of a three-track immigration policy.

A three-track immigration policy is proposed. As has been discussed earlier, Mainland-born children with the right of abode and their immediate family members should be admitted with no quota restriction under the first track. Under the second track, immigrants for family reunion who are not eligible for the right of abode will be admitted subject to quotas. Immigrants admitted under these first two tracks will contribute to the general labour supply of the economy. In recent years, because of the emphasis placed upon family reunion, the proportion of women and young children among new immigrants increased, and the labour force participation rate fell (see Chapter 4). The immediate contribution to the supply of labour in the Hong Kong labour market has been reduced, even though contribution in the long term can be sustained, as the immigrant children will grow up and enter the labour force. Any short-term shortfall in the general labour supply or bottlenecks in the labour market for professional and skilled personnel can be addressed by the immigration of skilled workers under the third track.

Given the low rate of natural population growth in Hong Kong, immigration has been the primary source of population growth and increase in the labour force (see Chapter 5). Immigration increases the general labour supply. Furthermore, an immigration policy that is targeted toward the admission of highly skilled immigrants can relieve bottlenecks that may emerge in the market for skilled workers and professionals, and hence will promote economic growth.

An estimation of an aggregate production function of Hong Kong from 1966 to 1990 by Lau (1994) shows the following elasticities of output:

Labour elasticity:	0.399
Human capital elasticity:	0.423
Capital elasticity:	0.465

In other words, a 1% increase in the labour input will increase the Gross Domestic Product (GDP) by 0.399%. Correspondingly, a 1% increase in human capital will increase the GDP by 0.423%. These figures mean that a substantial flow of immigrants that helps to maintain growth in the labour force will contribute significantly to economic growth. If the immigrants are educated and skilled, the contribution will be even larger.

Under the third track, skilled and professional personnel will be admitted outside the quota through a number of subsidiary schemes. Admission will be outside the quota so as to give flexibility in expanding or closing the schemes in order to adjust to the manpower situation in the labour market. At present, there are three subsidiary schemes for outside-quota immigration of skilled and professional personnel from the Mainland or of Mainland origin (see Chapter 3):

1. Chinese citizens originally from the Mainland who are now living overseas,

2. Employees of enterprises of Chinese capital from the Mainland, and
3. Mainland Chinese who hold degrees from thirty-six designated universities in the Mainland.

Among the three schemes, the third one has not been successful. Three years after its approval, the quota of 1,000 such Mainland graduates has not been fully taken up (Chapter 3). In the following section we propose an alternative supplementary scheme.

Allowing Mainland Graduates from Hong Kong Universities to Stay and Work

Proposal 10

Mainland students who graduate from local universities in Hong Kong should be allowed to stay and work in Hong Kong after graduation. They should be given employment visas if they are employed by local employers, and they should be granted permanent residence after seven years.

The third scheme above to import 1,000 professional and technical personnel is fraught with problems such as high recruitment costs, difficulty in identifying suitable candidates through agencies, and delays in bureaucratic processing of sponsorship (see Chapter 3). While the recruitment is taking place and applications are being processed, the candidates are in the Mainland, and this makes interviewing and communication difficult. Employers often have to rely heavily on recruitment agencies as intermediaries. Further, since the Hong Kong government wants to avoid fraud and circumvention of the quota system, it screens applications carefully to try to ensure that the candidates actually possess the skills required by the sponsoring local employers. All these problems and precautions could be eliminated if this scheme is replaced by one that allows Mainland students who graduate from universities in Hong Kong to stay and work on employment visas. The new scheme may require that they obtain employment that is relevant to their degree of studies from local employers within a specified period of, say, three months after graduation.

At present the University Grants Committee (UGC) allows local universities and UGC-funded institutions to admit students from the Mainland at both undergraduate and postgraduate levels.[2] Under the current policy, Mainland students are not allowed to stay in Hong Kong after graduation. They must return immediately to the Mainland upon completing their studies.

The proposed scheme has numerous advantages over the existing scheme of importing 1,000 professional and technical personnel. A highly subsidized university education in Hong Kong with the prospect of employment and residence afterwards should be sufficiently attractive to entice the best students in the Mainland. The stringent admission procedures of local universities will ensure that selection is by merit only and that the scheme will not be used as a back door by which to bring Mainland friends and relatives to Hong Kong to live. The strict bureaucratic screening of applications that the Hong Kong SAR government currently adopts for the existing scheme (No. 3) could be scrapped.

A strong argument in favour of our new scheme is that Mainland students who complete part of their education in Hong Kong will assimilate better into the economy and the community of Hong Kong than those imported Mainland professional and technical personnel. The rate of return to schooling acquired in Hong Kong is substantially higher than that acquired in the Mainland (see Chapter 7). It is economically more productive for Mainland students to attend universities in Hong Kong educational system than completing all their degrees in the Mainland prior to immigrating. Moreover, compared to the mature professionals who come to Hong Kong to work, Mainland students will be younger when they come to Hong Kong for university education. They are likely to adjust to a new social environment faster than those imported employees. For instance, they will have more time to learn the Cantonese dialect before starting to work. The prospective employers will also have the advantage of being able to interview job candidates before offering them employment. Under the present scheme, interviewing cost is generally very high (see Chapter 3).

The proposed scheme has still another advantage in that it contains a self-adjustment mechanism to market demand for skilled personnel. If market demand is weak, some of the Mainland graduates of local universities will not be able to find relevant employment within the specified period after graduation. Their visas will expire, and they will have to return to the Mainland. On the other hand, if they find employment readily after or even before graduation, it is a signal that there is a strong demand for the skill that they possess. In the case, the scheme could be expanded to permit local universities to allow Mainland students to make up a larger percentage of annual intake.

There may be a concern that Mainland students will take away jobs and lower the wage of local university graduates. Our analysis in Chapter 6, however, shows that the effect of immigrants, except for a massive influx, would likely be small in the short term and certainly negligible in the medium to long term.

If UGC-funded institutions admit non-local students up to the maximum percentage allowed by the UGC, and if non-local students are all from the Mainland, then there could be a total of about 1,800 of them in undergraduate degree programmes, 210 in taught Master's programmes, and 1,080 in research Master's or Ph.D. programmes. Since it is better to admit Mainland students at a young age, it is preferable to have more undergraduate than postgraduate Mainland students. Currently, there are more postgraduate than undergraduate students. Many local universities admit non-local postgraduate research students (mostly from the Mainland) up to or close to the percentage allowed by the UGC but so far have admitted virtually no undergraduate student from the Mainland. The reason is simply one of cost. Postgraduate research students are almost all supported by graduate assistantships and postgraduate studentships. Non-local undergraduate students, on the other hand, receive no financial support. The tuition fee and the living expenses in Hong Kong are beyond the means of almost all students from the Mainland without financial support. Local universities are trying to raise funds for scholarship support for Mainland students admitted into undergraduate programmes.

In the longer term, when financial support is secured, there will be room to increase the percentage of non-local undergraduate students admitted to local universities. Increasing the intake of Mainland undergraduates will not reduce local students' chances if the former are admitted outside the UGC student intake quota. Even if some of the increase is absorbed within the quota, it is socially more efficient to admit more Mainland students than local students because it is well known that some UGC-funded institutions have difficulty filling their admission quotas with qualified local students. The Mainland students admitted are likely to be of higher academic ability than those local students admitted at the margin. As long as the increase in the allowed percentage of non-local students within quota is moderate, there should not be a serious problem of displacement of qualified local students. Local universities could also take the opportunity to raise their current admission standards, which in some programmes are rather low. Places not taken up by local students because of the raised standards could then be taken up by qualified Mainland students. The UGC should give local universities more flexibility to adjust the intake mix of local and non-local students.

Conclusion on the Immigration Policy

In this concluding chapter, we draw on the research findings of previous chapters to support our proposals for changing the immigration policy. We propose a three-track immigration policy:

1. Admission (outside quota) of Mainland-born children with the right of abode and their immediate family members at any time they choose,
2. Admission (under quota) of other immigrants with top priority given to immediate family members of Hong Kong residents, and

3. Admission (outside quota) of skilled manpower from anywhere in the world, with the volume of admission aligned to the changing economic demand.

We argue that Hong Kong needs a substantial immigrant flow to maintain its population, its labour force, and, ultimately, its economic growth; and that it is economically beneficial to admit child immigrants as soon as possible and other immigrants when they are young. We supplement our economic arguments with historical arguments on the immigrant origin of the community; with social arguments on the costs of divided families; with humanitarian arguments on the values of family reunion; and with legal arguments on the letter and spirit of the Basic Law.

Immigration is very important to Hong Kong. Indeed, it is too important to be left to Immigration Department officials who execute orders. Yet, most people are probably unaware that an immigration policy does exist. Still fewer of them are aware of the rationale and the objectives behind the policy. It is one of the few examples of policy making in the public domain in which consultation and transparency are woefully absent. Every effort should be made to bring the policy out in the open for discussion, consultation, and debate. More research needs to be done to inform this debate so as to leave little room for hostility and fear mongering. Unfortunately such emotions have coloured the public opinion of child immigration in the months before the changeover on 1 July 1997.

Notes

1. Suen (1997) also proposes the idea of immediate admission of child immigrants with the right of abode. For a similar idea, see Wong (1997).

2. Universities in Hong Kong are all funded by the Government through the UGC. They are given quotas of total intake of students. At present, 2% of undergraduate and post-graduate students within the student target and 2% outside the target can come from non-local sources; but such postgraduate students must be in "taught" programmes as opposed to being "research students". In addition, up to thirty per cent of postgraduate research students can be from non-local sources.

Appendix A

Earnings Regression of Hong Kong Natives and Immigrants

(Pre-1981 Arrival Cohort, 1981 and 1996)

	1981		1996	
	Natives	Immigrants	Natives	Immigrants
Constant	6.0001	6.6841	7.5095	8.4036
	(759.562)	(884.144)	(986.825)	(618.001)
S	0.0954	0.0457	0.1131	0.0594
	(190.577)	(107.248)	(272.050)	(89.807)
EXP	0.0680	0.0345	0.0569	0.0200
	(129.520)	(72.895)	(132.306)	(28.107)
EXP^2	−0.00105	−0.00055	−0.00084	−0.00036
	(−97.441)	(−69.952)	(−91.156)	(−31.256)
R^2	0.3266	0.1481	0.3789	0.2024
N	86,685	109,943	131,851	57,818

Source: Sample data from Hong Kong Census 1981 and By-census 1996.

Note: t-statistics in parentheses, S = years of schooling, EXP = years of experience, EXP^2 = years of experience squared, N = sample size.

Appendix B*

Decomposition of Earnings Inequality

The variance of logarithmic earnings of a population V with k groups is given by

$$V = \frac{1}{n} \sum_{i=1}^{k} \sum_{j} n_{ij} \left(x_{ij} - x_{..} \right)^2$$

$$= \sum_{i} \left(\frac{n_i}{n} \right) V_i + \sum_{i} \frac{n_i}{n} \left(x_{i.} - x_{..} \right)^2 \cdots\cdots\cdots\cdots\cdots (8.1)$$

where

x_{ij} = log earnings of jth individual in the ith population group
$x_{i.}$ = mean of log earnings of the ith population group
$x_{..}$ = mean of log earnings of the entire population
n_i = number of individuals in the ith population group
n = number of individuals in the entire population
V_i = variance of log earnings of the ith population group.

Equation (8.1) shows that the inequality measure is made up of two components: within-group inequality V_w and between-group inequality V_B where

$$V_w \equiv \sum_{i} \left(\frac{n_i}{n} \right) V_i$$

$$V_B \equiv \sum_{i} \frac{n_i}{n} \left(x_{i.} - x_{..} \right)^2$$

The within-group inequality is a result of the aggregate contribution of log earnings variance within each heterogeneous group weighted by the respective population share $(\frac{n_i}{n})$.

The between-group inequality is a result of the presence of heterogeneous groups that have mean log earnings different from the population mean. The variance of the difference in group mean and the population mean is also weighted, respectively, by the population share to give the between-group inequality.

Any change in overall earnings inequality over time can be represented by the sum of changes in within-group inequality and between-group inequality, each of which in turn can be decomposed. For instance, a change in within-group inequality from 1981 to 1996 can be decomposed as follows (See Karoly, 1992):

$$V_w^{96} - V_w^{81} = \sum_{i=1}^{k} (\frac{n_i}{n})^{96} V_i^{96} - \sum_{i=1}^{k} (\frac{n_i}{n})^{81} V_i^{81}$$

$$= \sum_{i} (\frac{n_i}{n})^{81} (V_i^{96} - V_i^{81}) + \sum_{i} \left[(\frac{n_i}{n})^{96} - (\frac{n_i}{n})^{81} \right] V_i^{81}$$

$$+ \ interaction\ term \cdots\cdots\cdots\cdots\cdots\cdots (8.2)$$

The first term on the right-hand side is caused by a change in earnings dispersion among the k population groups, using 1981 group shares as weights. The second term is caused by a change in group shares, using 1981 log earnings variance as weights. The third term is the interaction term. A similar decomposition can be performed using 1996 group shares and the log earnings variance as weights. This procedure of decomposition enables us to separate the effect (on earnings inequality) of a change in group shares from the effect of a change in earnings dispersion.

Note:

* See Chapter 8 for explanation and application.

Appendix C*

Human Capital Model of Earnings Inequality

The relation between investments in human capital and earnings is represented by the well-known Mincerian earnings function (Mincer, 1974) as follows:

$$\log Y = \log Y_0 + rS + \alpha X + \beta X^2 \cdots\cdots\cdots\cdots\cdots (8.3)$$

where Y is the earnings, S the years of schooling, r the rate of return to schooling, X the years of experience, and Y_0 the earnings when both S and X are zero.

Using a decomposition by Goodman (1960) and assuming that r and S, and α and X, are uncorrelated, we have

$$\mathrm{var}\ (\log Y) = \bar{r}^{\,2}\ \mathrm{var}\ (S) + \bar{S}^{\,2}\ \mathrm{var}\ (r) + \mathrm{var}\ (S)\ \mathrm{var}\ (r)$$

$$+ \bar{\alpha}^{\,2}\ \mathrm{var}\ (X) + \bar{X}^{\,2}\ \mathrm{var}\ (\alpha)$$

$$+ \mathrm{var}\ (X)\ \mathrm{var}\ (\alpha) + \mathrm{other\ terms} \cdots\cdots (8.4)$$

where a bar denotes the mean value.

If we ignore variations in the rate of return to schooling r and α across individuals, then, *ceteris paribus*, variance in log earnings, or in other words dispersion in earnings, will depend on the variance of years of schooling and years of experience across individuals. It is clear then, *ceteris paribus*, that an increase in earnings inequality over time is driven by increasing variance in years of schooling and experience and possibly by increasing rates of return to schooling and experience.

Note:

* See Chapter 8 for explanation and application.

Bibliography

1. Altonji, Joseph G., and Card, David (1991). "The Effects of Immigration on the Labor Market Outcomes of Less-Skilled Natives," in *Immigration, Trade and the Labor Market*, John M. Abowd and Richard B. Freeman, eds. Chicago: University of Chicago Press, pp. 201–234.

2. Anand, Sudhir (1983). *Inequality and Poverty in Malaysia: Measurement and Decomposition*. Oxford: Oxford University Press.

3. Baker, Michael, and Benjamin, Dwayne (1993). "The Receipt of Transfer Payments by Immigrants in Canada." Toronto: University of Toronto. (mineo.)

4. _____ (1994). "The Performance of Immigrants in the Canadian Labor Market," *Journal of Labor Economics*, 12 (July): 369–405.

5. Bean, Frank D. Lowell, B. Lindsay, and Taylor, Lowell J. (1988). "Undocumented Mexican Immigrants and the Earnings of Other Workers in the United States," *Demography*, vol. 25. No. 1 (February): 35–52.

6. Becker, Gary S. (1964). *Human Capital*. New York: Columbia University Press.

7. _____ (1967). *Human Capital and the Personal Distribution of Income: An Analytic Approach*. Woytinsky Lecture 13, Institute of Public Administration, University of Michigan, Ann Arbor.

8. _____ (1981). *A Treatise on the Family*. Cambridge: Harvard University Press.

9. Blau, Francine (1984). "The Use of Transfer Payments by Immigrants," *Industrial Labor Relations Review*, vol. 37. No. 2 (January): 222–239.

10. Bloom, David E., and Gunderson, M. (1991). "An Analysis of the Earnings of Canadian Immigrants," in *Immigration, Trade and the Labor Market*, Abowd, John M. and Freeman, Richard B., eds. Chicago: University of Chicago Press, pp. 321–342.

11. Bloom, David E., Grenier, G., and Gunderson, M. (1994). "The Changing Labor Market Position of Canadian Immigration," *NBER Working Paper No. 4672* (March), Cambridge: National Bureau of Economic Research.

12. Borjas, George J. (1985). "Assimilation, Changes in Cohort Quality, and the Earnings of Immigrants," *Journal of Labor Economics*, 3 (October): 463–489.

167

13. Borjas, George J. (1986). "The Sensitivity of Labor Demand Function to Choice of Dependent Variables," *Review of Economics and Statistics*, 68.1 (February): 58–66.

14. _____ (1990). *Friends or Strangers: The Impact of Immigrants on the U.S. Economy*. New York: Basic Books.

15. _____ (1994). "The Economics of Immigration," *Journal of Economic Literature*, 32.4 (December): 1,667–1,717.

16. _____ (1995). "The Economic Benefits from Immigration," *Journal of Economic Perspectives*, vol. 9. No. 2 (Spring): 3–22.

17. _____ (1995). "Assimilation and Changes in Cohort Quality Revisited: What Happened to Immigrant Earnings in the 1980s?" *Journal of Labor Economics*, 13 (April): 201–245.

18. Borjas, George J., Freeman, Richard B., and Katz, Lawrence F. (1992). "On the Labor Market Effects of Immigration and Trade," in *Immigration and The Work Force: Economic Consequences for the United States and Source Areas*, George J. Borjas and Richard B. Freeman, eds. Chicago: University of Chicago Press, pp. 212–244.

19. Borjas, George J., and Tienda, Marta (1987). "The Economic Consequences of Immigration," *Science*, 235 (February): 645–651.

20. Cain, G. (1976). "The Challenge of Segmented Labor Market Theories to Orthodox Theory: A Survey," *Journal of Economic Literature*, vol. 14. No. 4 (December): 1,215–1,257.

21. Card, David (1990). "The Impact of Mariel Boatlift on the Miami Labor Market," *Industrial Labor Relations Review*, vol. 43. No. 2 (January): 245–257.

22. Chiswick, B. R. (1978). "The Effect of Americanization on the Earnings of Foreign-Born Men," *Journal of Political Economy*, 86: 893–921.

23. Chung, Yue-Ping; Ho, Lok-Sang; and Liu, Pak-Wai (1994). "An Economic Analysis of Continuing Education: Costs, Benefits, Trends, and Issues." (August), Hong Kong: University and Polytechnic Grants Committee.

24. Dustmann, C. (1993). "Earnings Adjustment of Temporary Migrants," *Journal of Population Economics*, 6: 153–168.

25. Ehrenberg, Ronald G., and Smith, Robert S. (1991). *Modern Labor Economics: Theory and Public Policy*. New York: Harper Collins.

26. Filer, Randall K. (1992). "The Effect of Immigrant Arrivals on Migratory Patterns of Native Workers," in *Immigration and the Work Force: Economic Consequences for the United States and Source Areas*, George

J. Borjas and Richard B. Freeman, eds. Chicago: University of Chicago Press, pp. 245–269.

27. Frey, William H (1994). "The New White Flight," *American Demographics*, vol. 16. No. 4 (April): pp. 40–48.

28. Friedberg, Rachel, M., and Hunt, Jennifer (1995). "The Impact of Immigrants on Host Country Wages, Employment and Growth," *Journal of Economic Perspectives*, vol. 9. No. 2 (Spring): 25–44.

29. Goodman, Leo (1960). "On the Exact Variance of Products," *Journal of American Statistical Association*, 55 (December): 708–713.

30. Greenwood, Michael J., and McDowell, John M (1986). "The Factor Market Consequences of U.S. Immigration," *Journal of Economic Literature*, 24.4 (December): 1,738–1,772.

31. Grossman, Jean Baldwin (1982). "The Substitutability of Natives and Immigrants in Production," *Review of Economic Statistics*, 64.4 (November): 596–603.

32. Ho, Lok Sang; Lam, Kit Chun; and Liu, Pak Wai (1991). "International Labour Migration: The Case of Hong Kong." *Occasional Paper No. 8* (September), The Hong Kong Institute of Asia-Pacific Studies, The Chinese University of Hong Kong.

33. Hong Kong Government. *Hong Kong Report*. Hong Kong, 1997

34. Karoly, Lynn A. (1992). "Changes in the Distribution of Individual Earnings in the United States: 1967–1986," *Review of Economics and Statistics*, vol. 74. No. 1 (February): 107–115.

35. Kono, Shigemi (1996). "Relation Between Women's Economic Activity and Child Care in Low-Fertility Countries," in United Nations, *Population and Women*, New York: United Nations.

36. Kwong, Paul C. K. (1993). "Internationalization of Population and Globalization of Families," in *The Other Hong Kong Report* 1993, Po-King Choi and Lok-Sang Ho, eds. Hong Kong: The Chinese University of Hong Kong Press, pp. 147–174.

37. LaLonde, Robert J., and Topel, Robert H. (1991). "Labor Market Adjustments to Increased Immigration," in *Immigration, Trade and the Labor Market*, John M. Abowd and Richard B. Freeman, eds. Chicago: University of Chicago Press, pp. 67–199.

38. _____ (1992). "The Assimilation of Immigrants in the U.S. Labor Market," in *Immigration and the Work Force: Economic Consequences for the United States and Source Areas*, George J. Borjas and Richard B. Freeman, eds. Chicago: University of Chicago Press, pp. 67–92.

39. Lam, Kit Chun (1986). "Imperfect Information, Specificity of Schooling and Rate of Return Migration," *Economic Letters*, 21: 280–283.

40. _____, Liu, Pak Wai (1996). "Change in Immigrant Cohorts and Their Economic Assimilation in a Rapidly Restructuring Economy," Department of Economics, The Chinese University of Hong Kong (May).

41. _____ (1997). "Earnings Divergence and Assimilation of Immigrants," *Working Paper No. 83* (August), Department of Economics, The Chinese University of Hong Kong.

42. _____ (1998). "Immigration, Population Heterogeneity and Earnings Inequality in Hong Kong," *Contemporary Economic Policy*, forthcoming.

43. Lau, Lawrence J. (1994). "Sources of Long-Term Economic Growth: Empirical Evidence from Developed and Developing Countries." Standford University (May).

44. Lin, Justin Yifu (1990). "Collectivisation and China's Agricultural Crisis in 1959–1961," *Journal of Political Economy*, vol. 98. No. 6 (December): 1,228–1,252.

45. Lin, Tzong-Biau (1995). "Growth, Equity, and Income Distribution Policies in Hong Kong," *The Developing Economics*, vol. 22. No. 4 (December): 391–413.

46. Liu, Pak Wai and Wong, Yue-Chim (1981). "Human Capital and Inequality in Singapore," *Economic Development and Cultural Change*, 29.2 (January): 275–293.

47. Mincer, Jacob (1974). *Schooling, Experience and Earnings*. New York: Columbia University Press.

48. Muller, Thomas, and Espenshade, Thomas J. (1985). *The Fourth Wave*. Washington, D.C.: Urban Institute Press.

49. Piore, M. (1979). *Birds of Passage: Migrant Labor and Industrial Societies*. Cambridge: Cambridge University Press.

50. Sen, Amartya (1973). *On Economic Inequality*. Oxford: Clarendon.

51. Simon, Julian, L. (1989). *The Economic Consequences of Immigration*. Cambridge, Massachusetts: Basil Blackwell.

52. Simon, Julian L., Moore, Stephen, and Sullivan, Richard (1993). "The Effect of Immigration on Aggregate Native Unemployment: An Across-City Estimation," *Journal of Labor Research*, vol. 14. No. 3 (Summer): 299–316.

53. Sjaastad, L. A. (1962). "The Costs and Returns of Human Migration," *Journal of Political Economy*, vol. 70. No. 5 (October): 80–93.

54. Skeldon, Ronald (1995). "Immigration and Population Issues," in *The Other Hong Kong Report 1995*, Stephen Y. L. Cheung and Stephen M. H. Sze, eds. Hong Kong: The Chinese University Press, pp. 303–316.

55. Suen, Wing (1993). "Sectoral Shifts: Impact on Hong Kong Workers." School of Economics and Finance, The University of Hong Kong (November).

56. _____ (1994). "Estimating the Effects of Immigration in One City," *Discussion Paper No. 159* (April), School of Economics and Finance, The University of Hong Kong.

57. _____ (1997). "A Two-Track Immigration Policy." *HKCER Letters*, 46 (September): 1–2.

58. White, Michael J., and Hunter, Lori (1993). "The Migratory Response of Native-Born Workers to the Presence of Immigrants in the Labor Market." Brown University (July).

59. Willis, R. (1973). "A New Approach to the Economic Theory of Fertility," *Journal of Political Economy*, 81.2 (March / April): 14–64.

60. Winegarden, C. R., and Khor, Lay Boon (1991). "Undocumented Immigration and Unemployment of U.S. Youth and Minority Workers: Econometric Evidence," *Review of Economics and Statistics*, vol. 73. No. 1 (February): 105–112.

61. Wong, Yue-Chim Richard (1997a). "Time to Count the Social Cost of a Divided People United," *South China Morning Post*, 19 May.

62. _____ (1997b). "Hong Kong Growing as Part of China: A Historical Perspective," Paper presented at Far Eastern Econometric Society Meeting, Hong Kong, 24–26 July.

63. _____ (1997c). "Mainland Immigrants Must Be Welcomed," Paper presented at International Asian Studies Programme 20th Anniversary Reunion Seminar on "Future of Hong Kong SAR within China and the Asian Region", The Chinese University of Hong Kong, Hong Kong (July).

Index

About the Authors

Kit Chun Lam, B.So.Sc., Chinese University of Hong Kong, M.A., Ph.D., Harvard University. She is Associate Professor at the Department of Economics, Hong Kong Baptist University. Professor Lam's research interest is in labour economics.

Pak Wai Liu, A.B., Princeton University and M.A., Ph.D., Stanford University. He is Professor of Economics and Pro-Vice-Chancellor, Chinese University of Hong Kong. Research Director, Hong Kong Centre for Economic Research; Co-Director, Hong Kong and Asia-Pacific Economies Research Programme, Hong Kong Institute of Asia-Pacific Studies; Secretary General of East Asian Economic Association. He is a part-time member of the Central Policy Unit and a member of the Economic Advisory Committee, the Industry and Technology Development Council, Services Support Fund Vetting Committee, the Commission on Strategic Development, the Chief Executive's Commission on Innovation and Technology, and the Task Force on Employment. Professor Liu's research focus is on labour economics and applied theory.

The Hong Kong Economic Policy Studies Series